CUTE CATS COLORING BOOK

FOR KIDS AGES 5-8

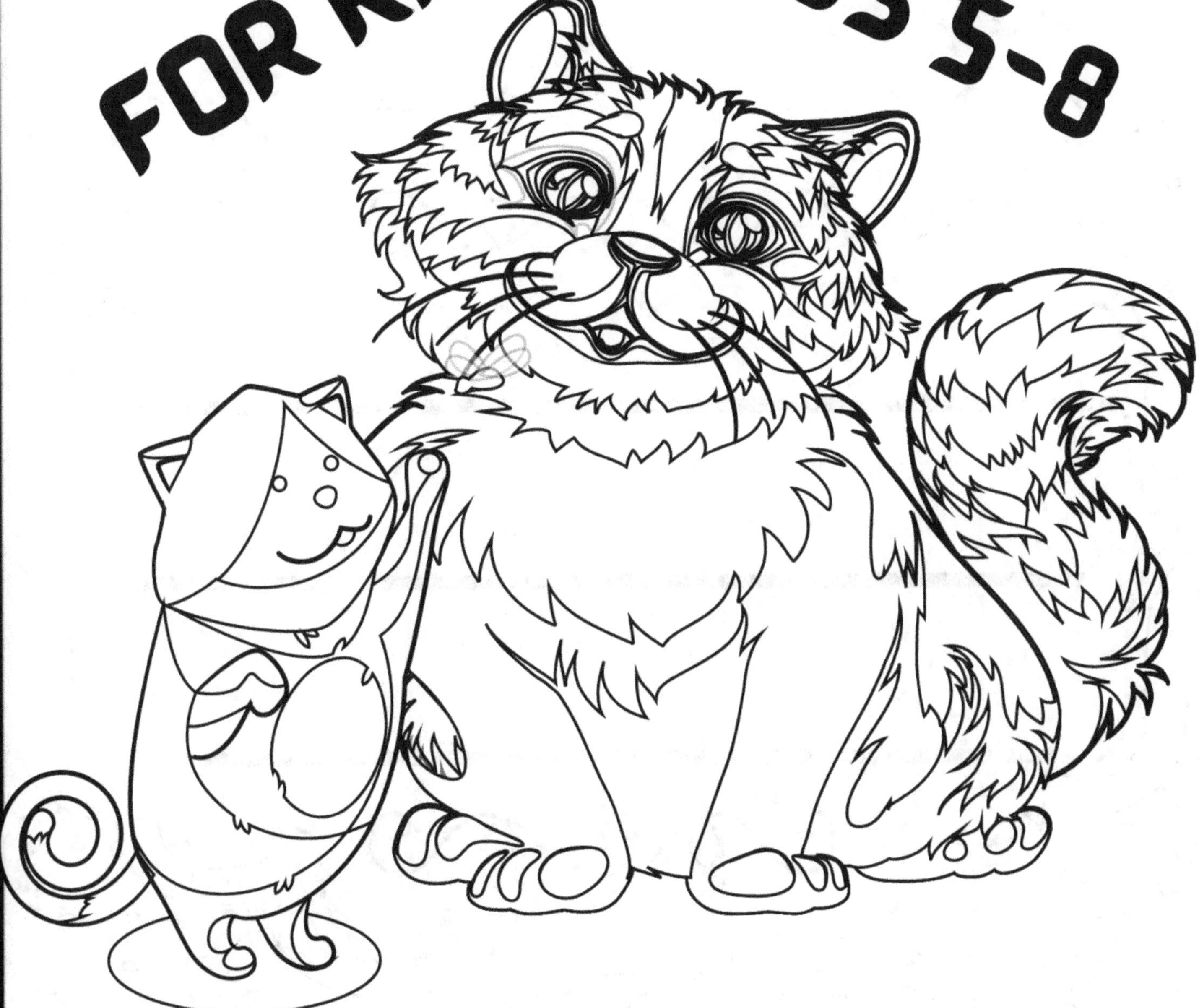

THIS BOOK BELONG TO

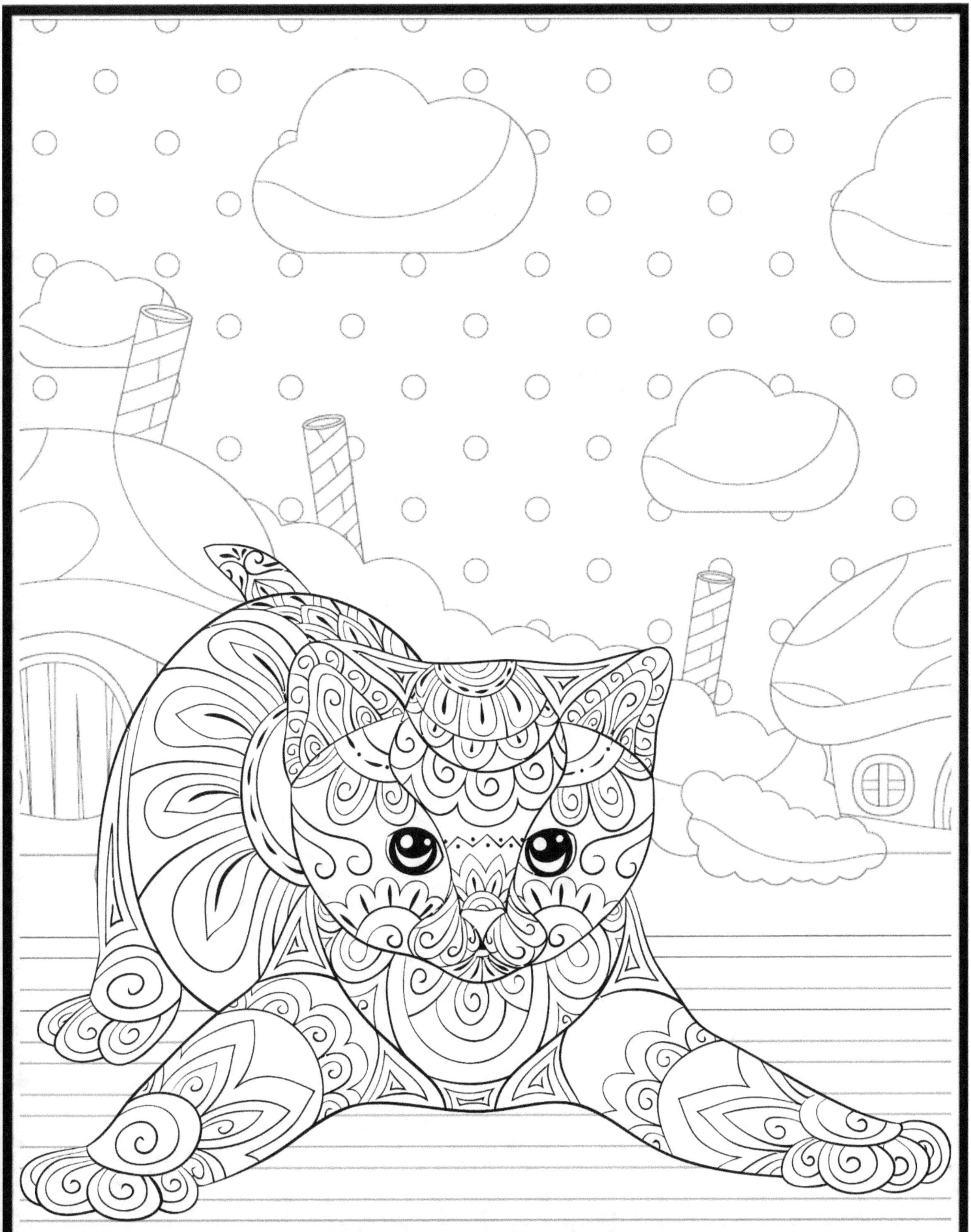

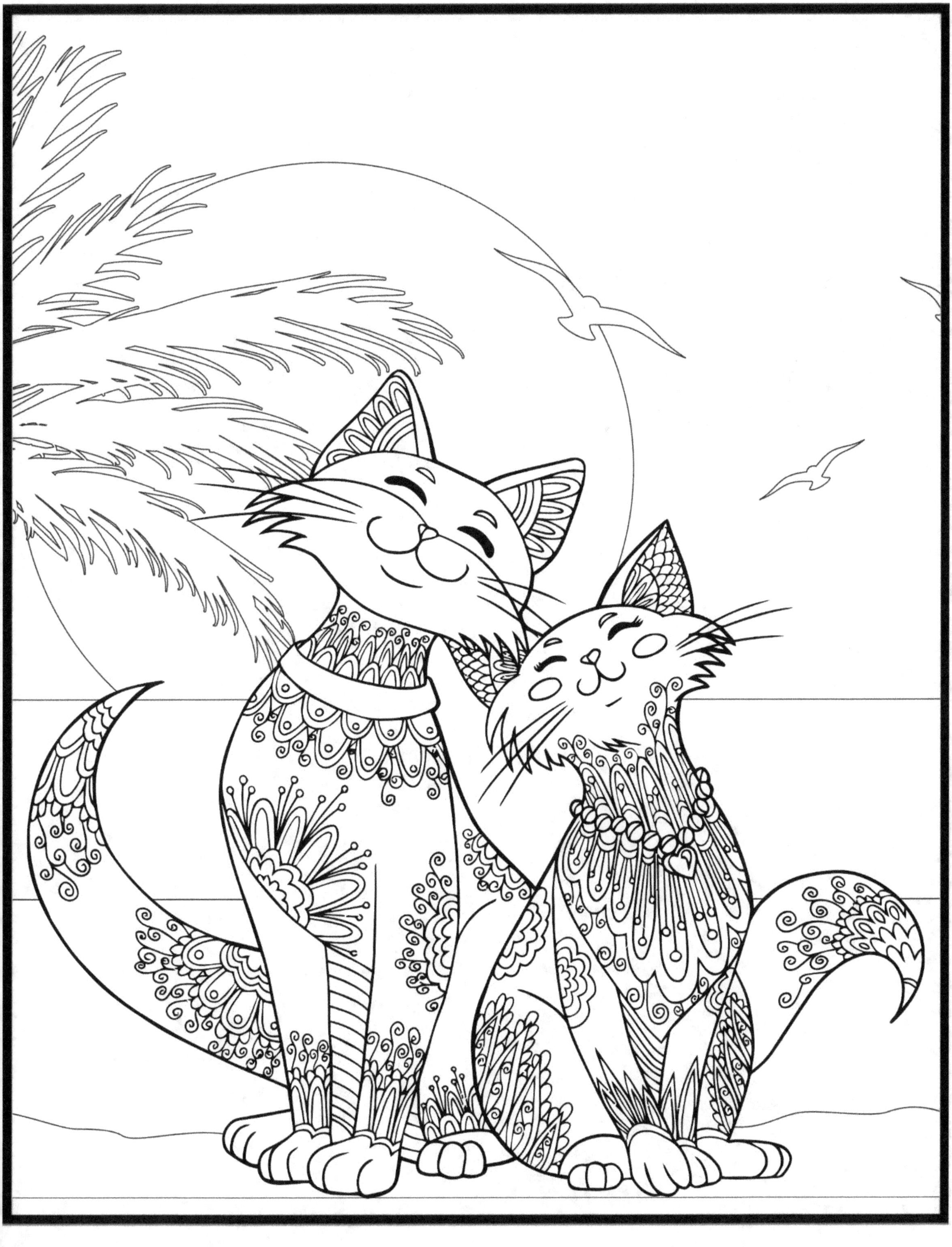

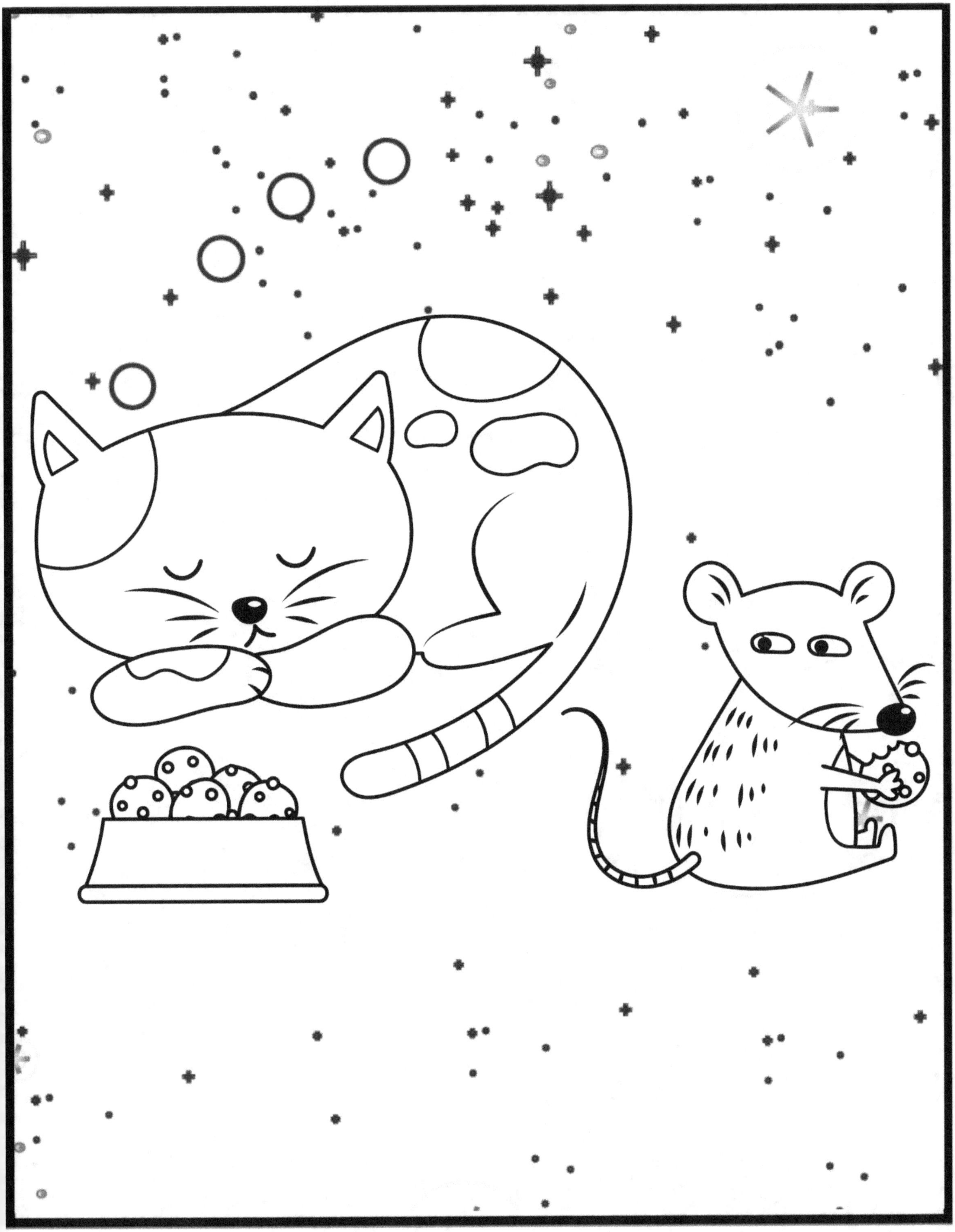

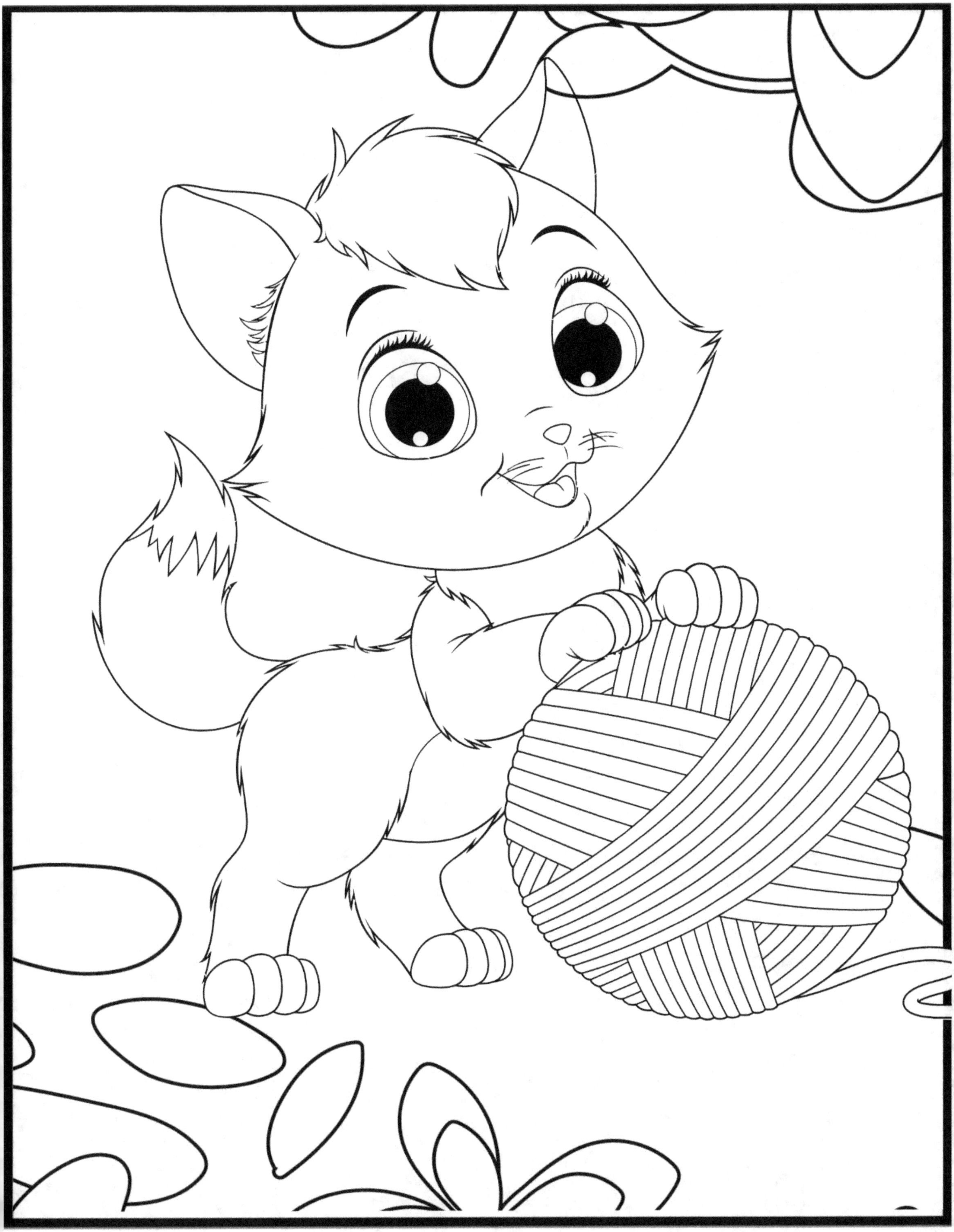

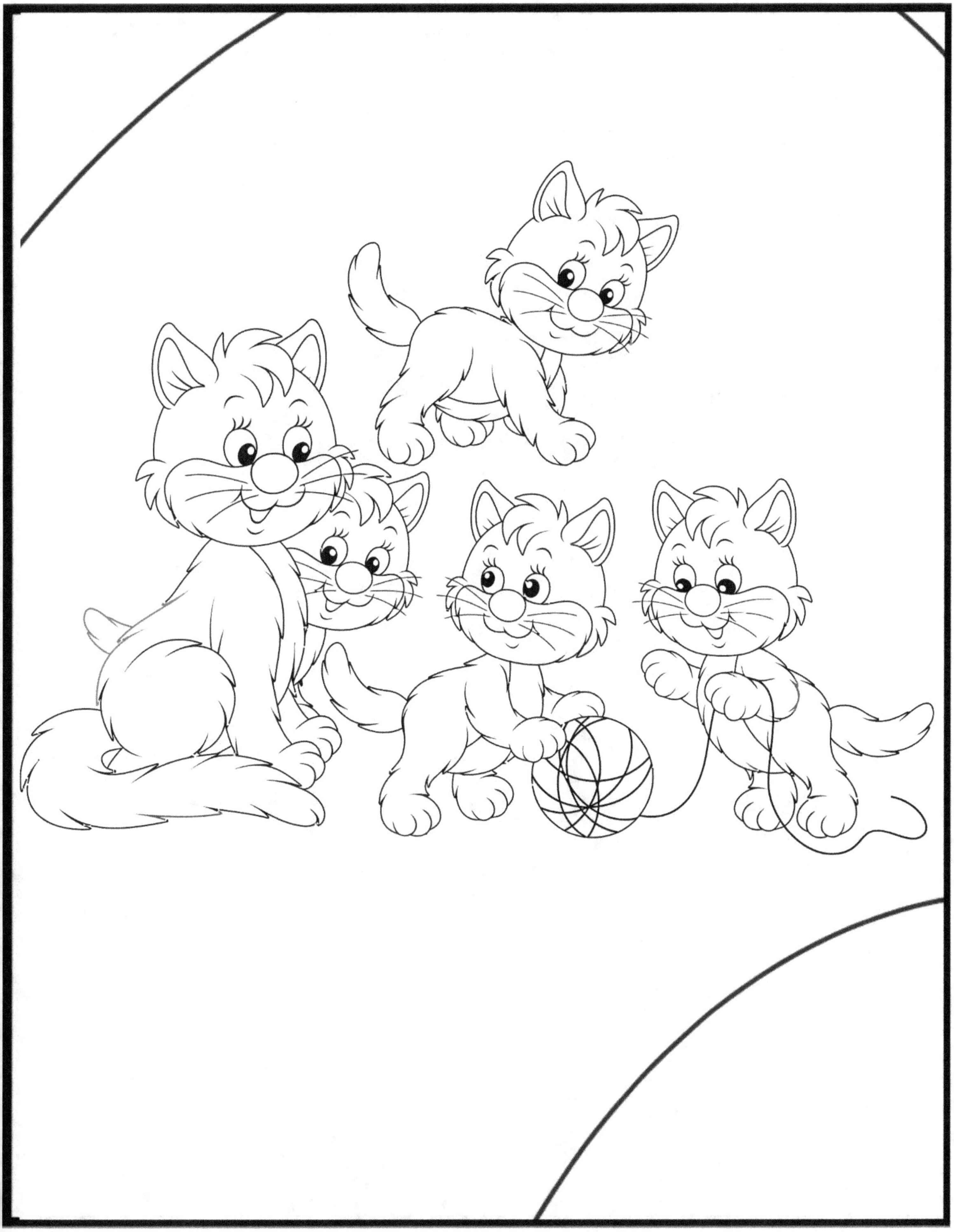

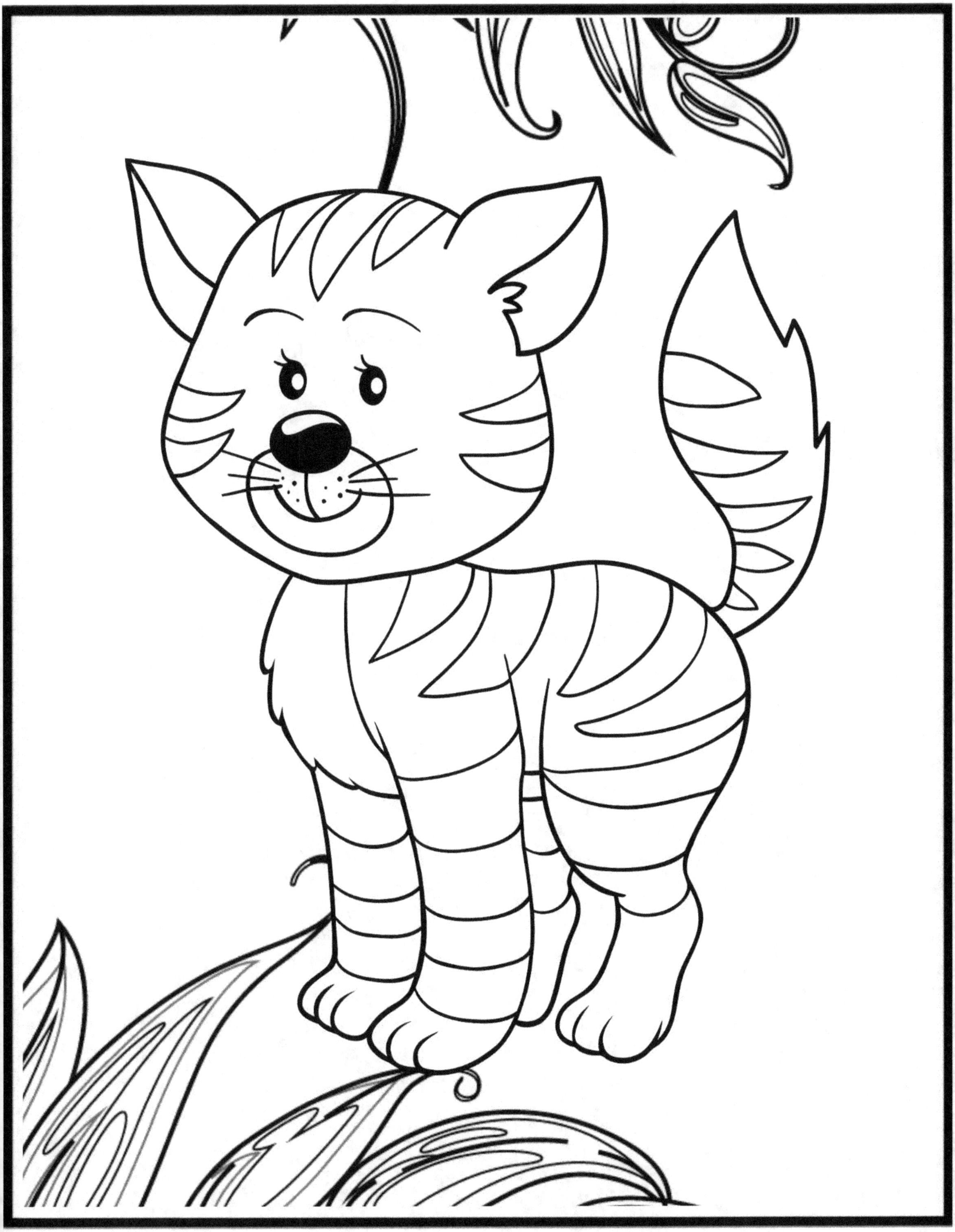

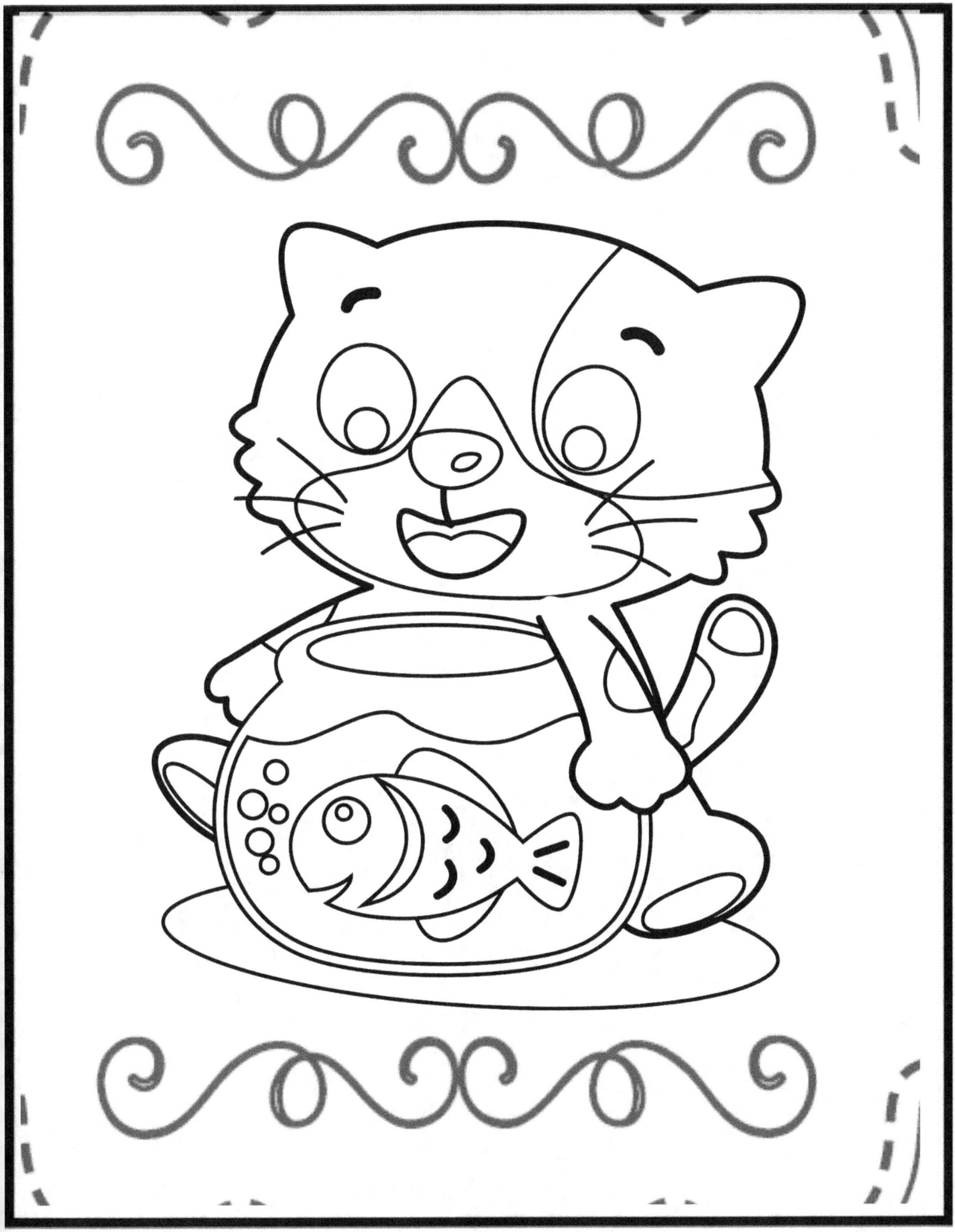

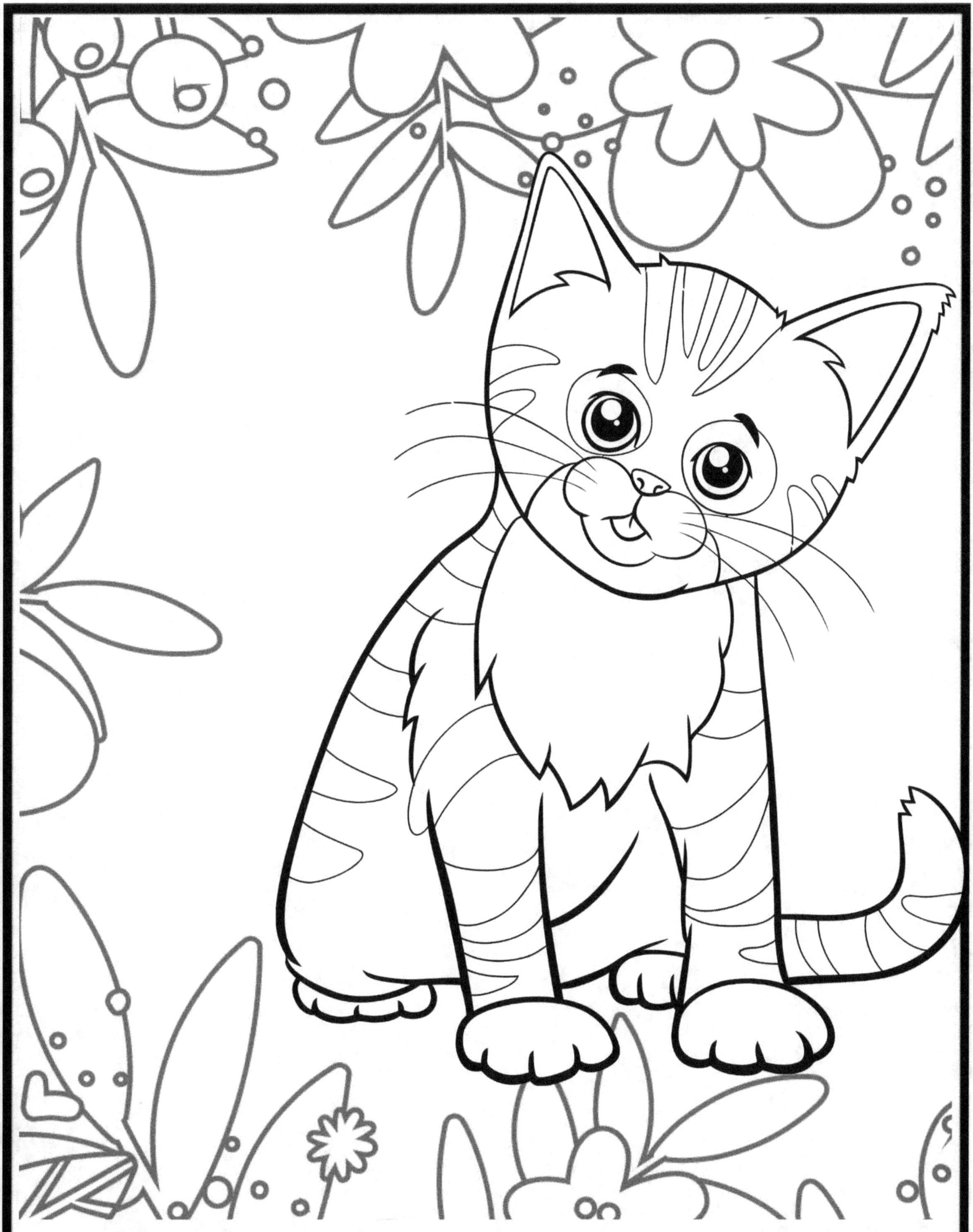

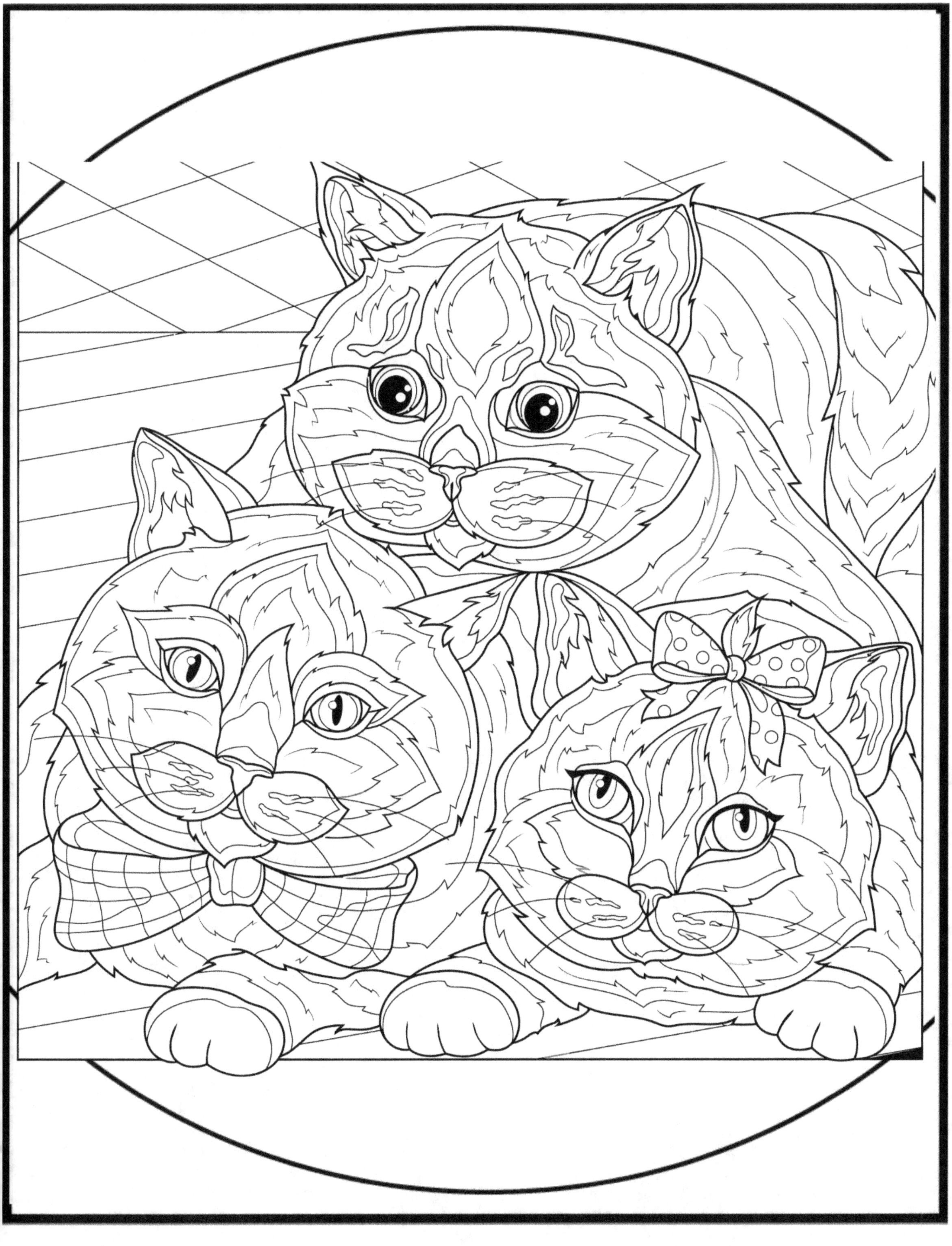

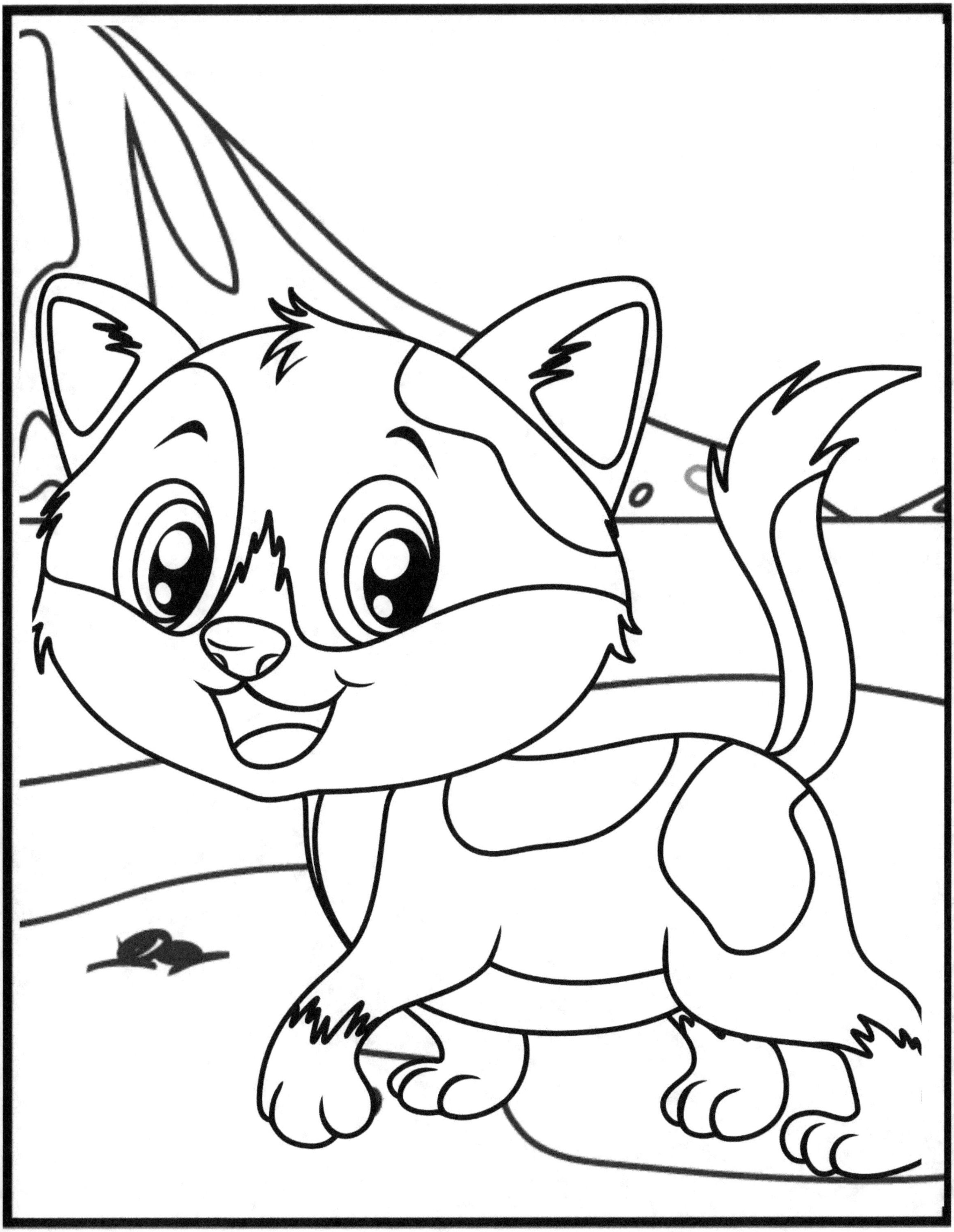

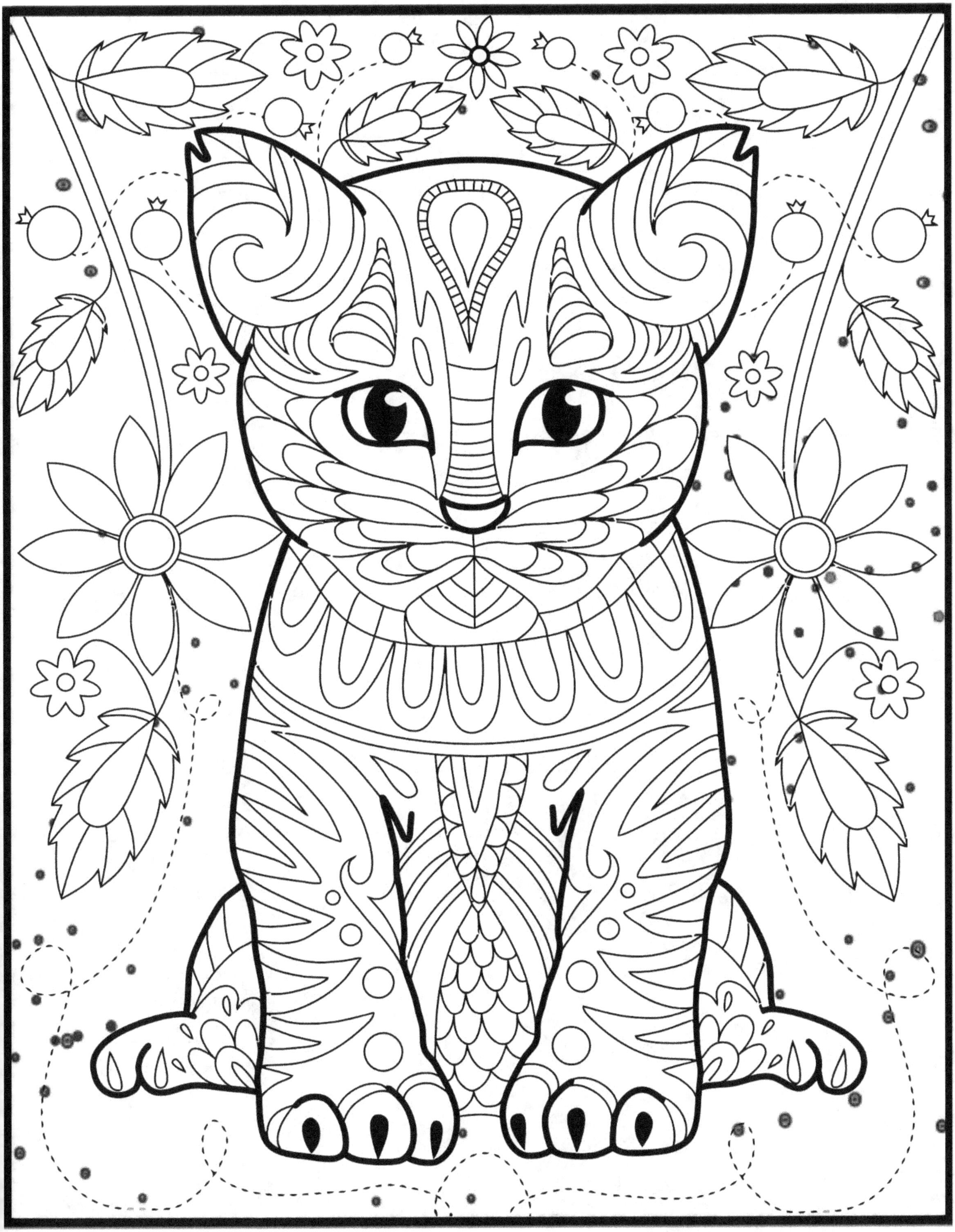

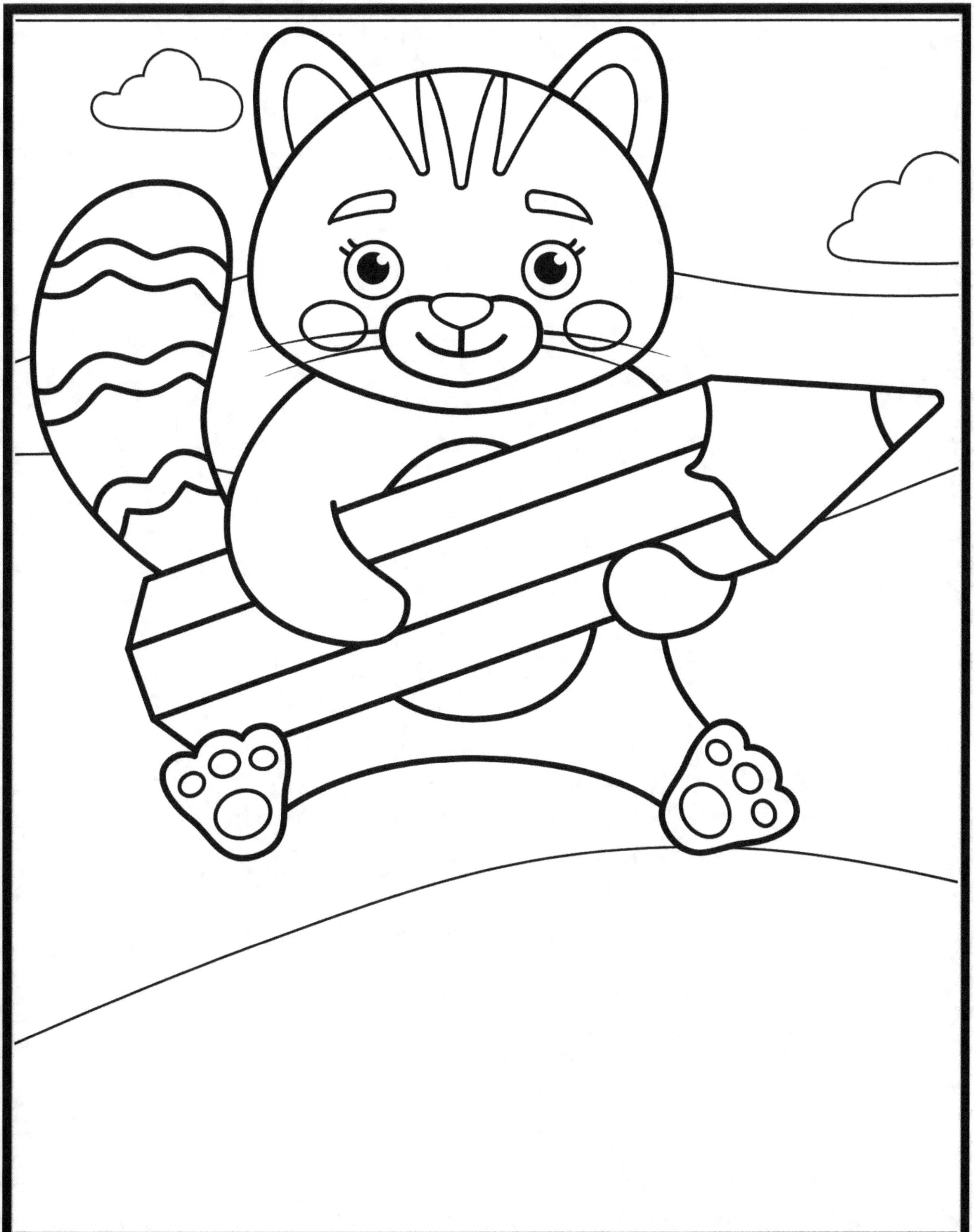

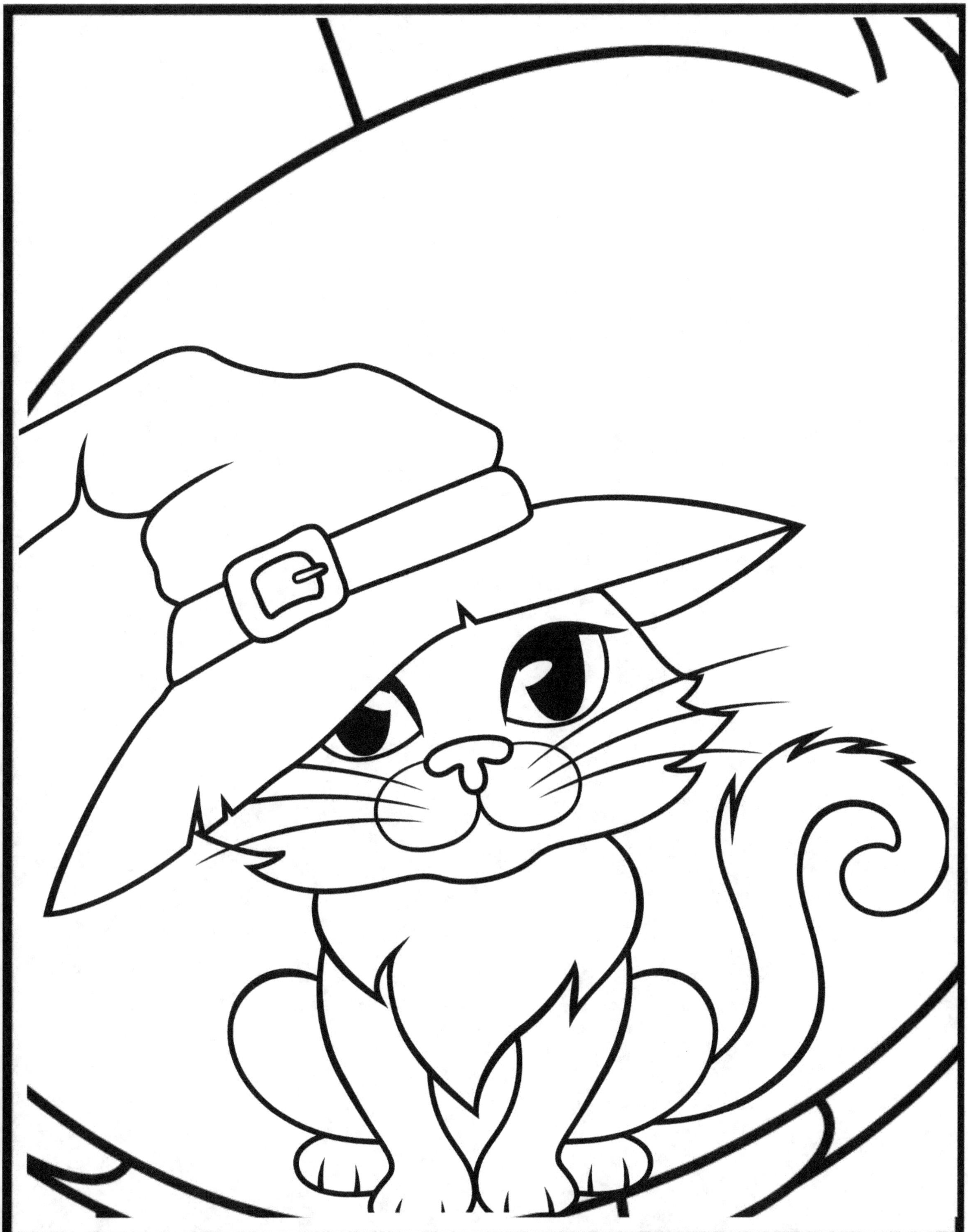

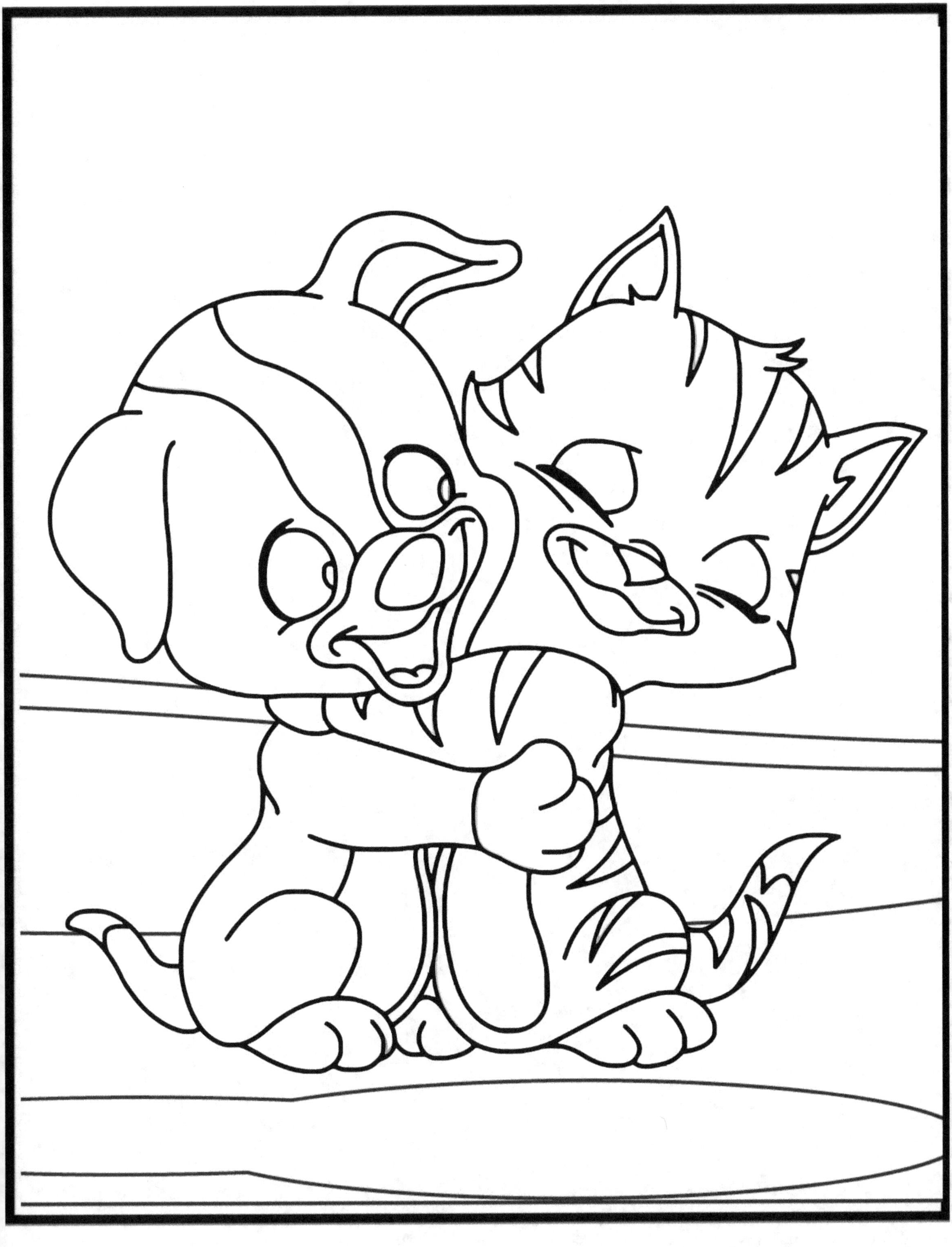

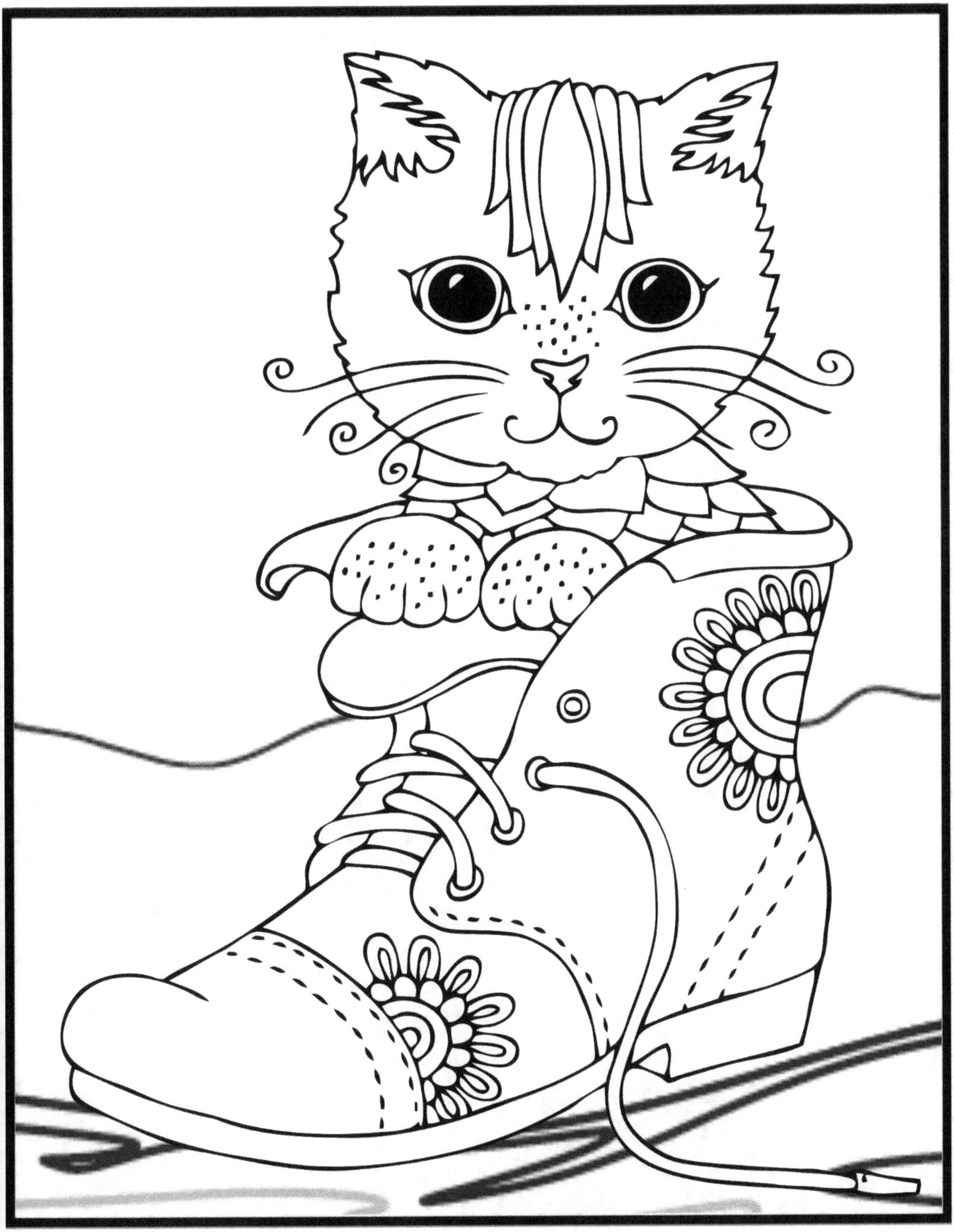

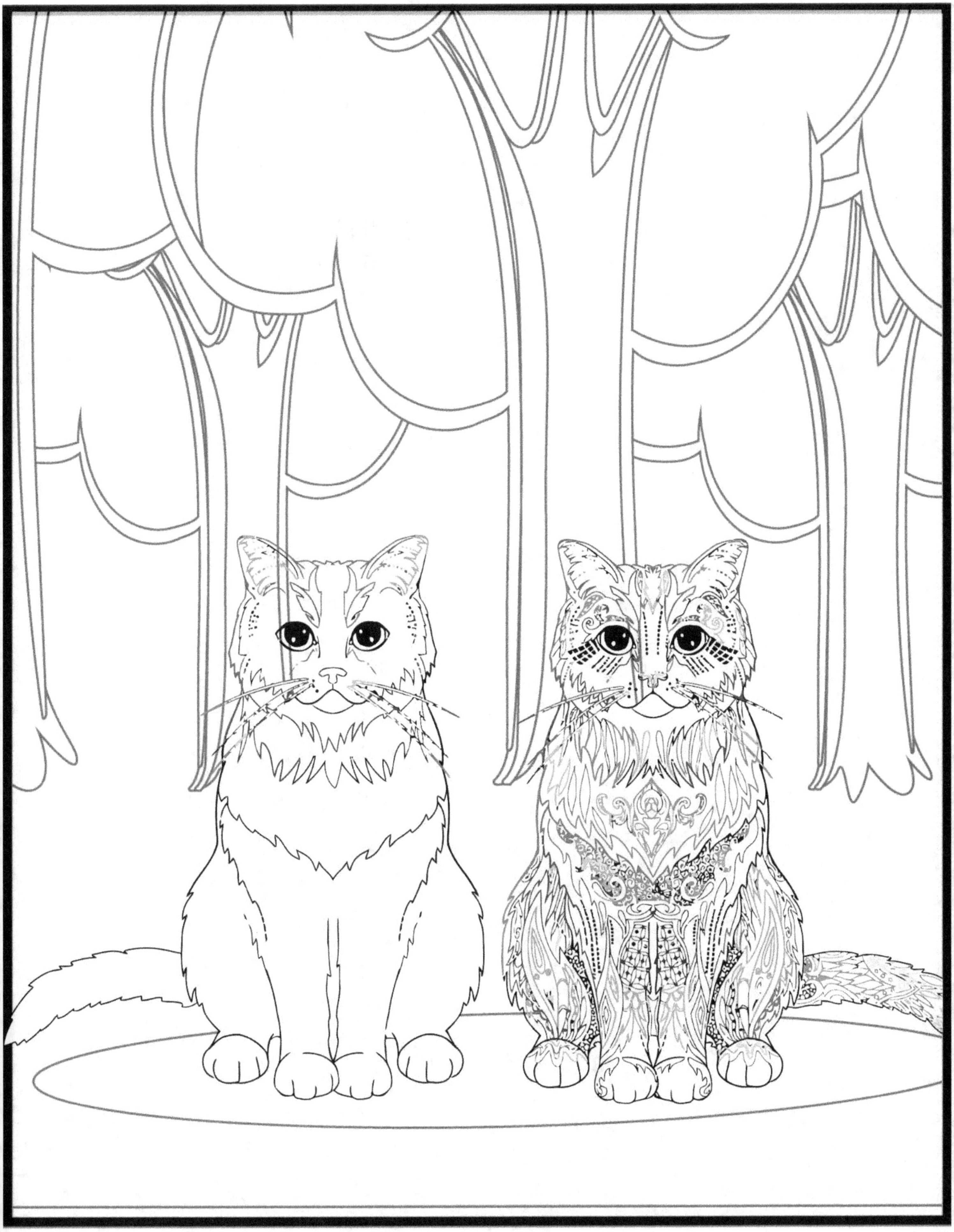

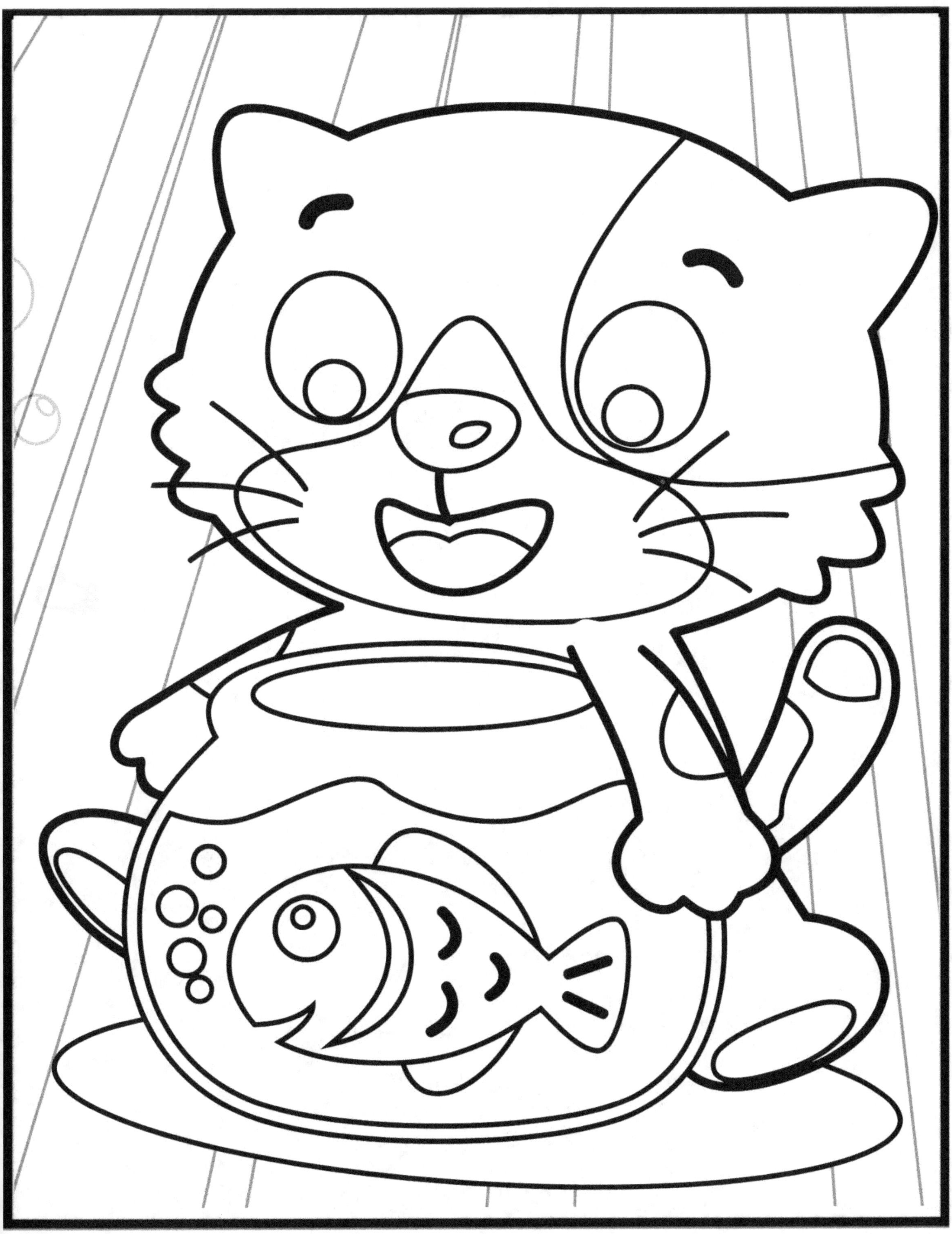

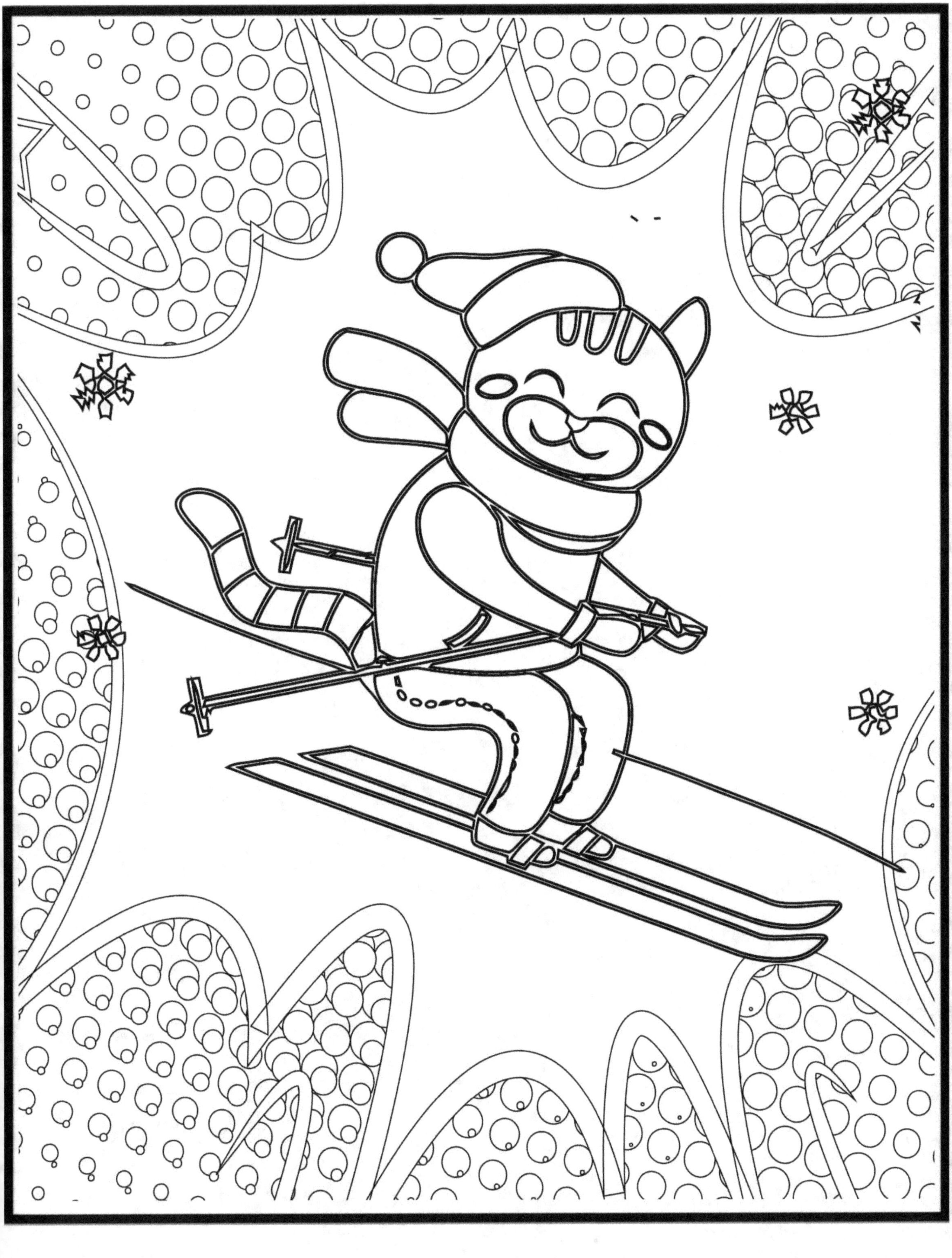

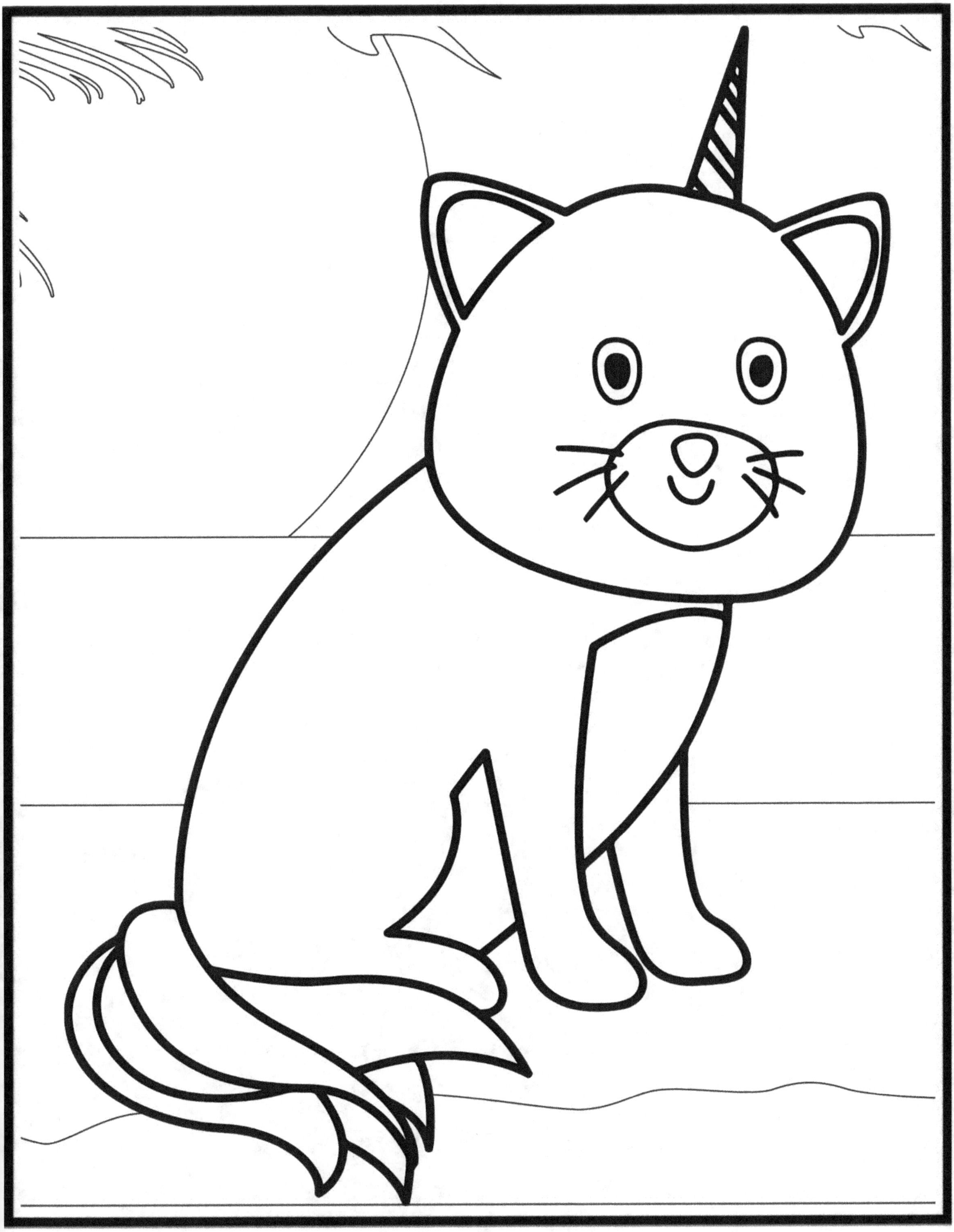

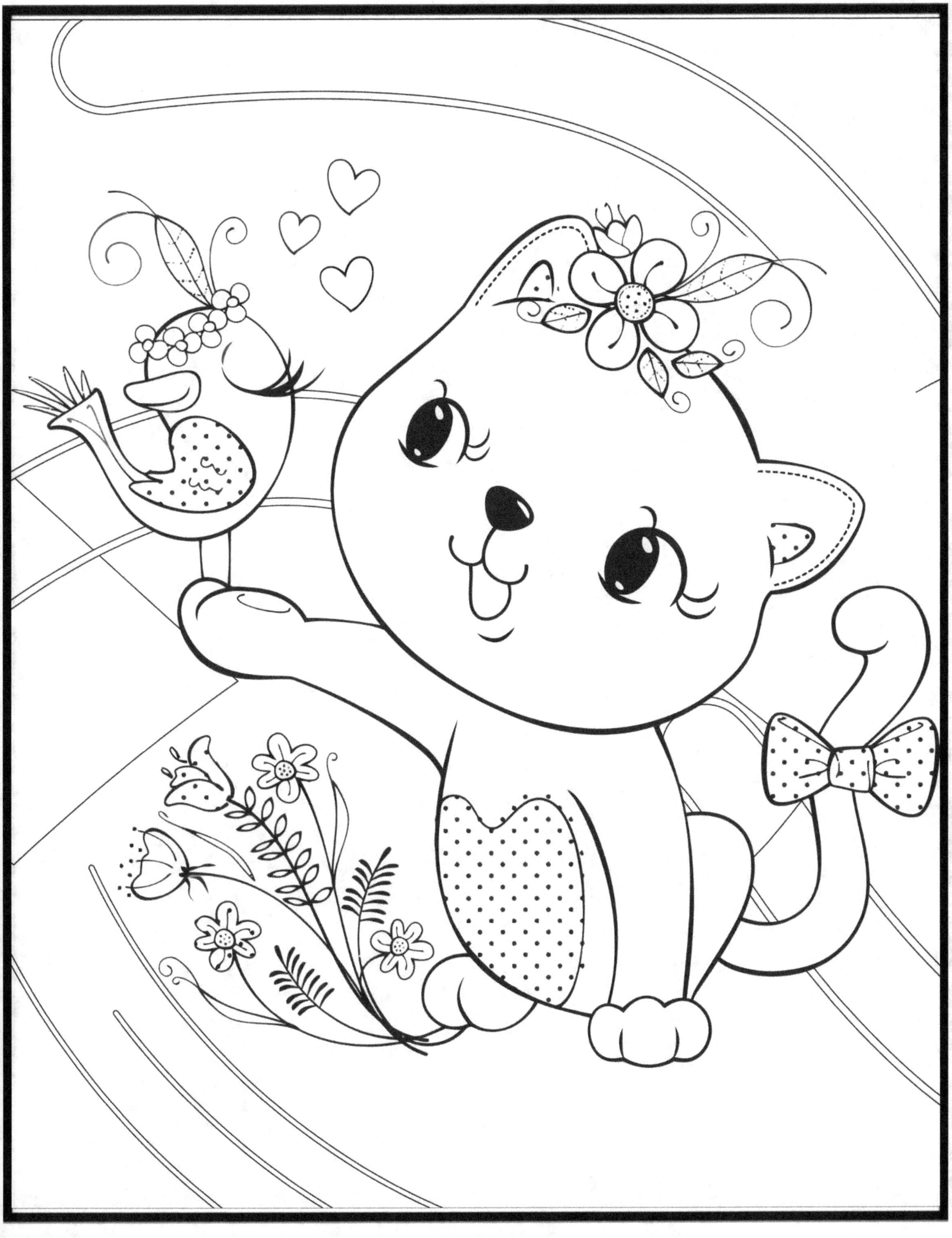

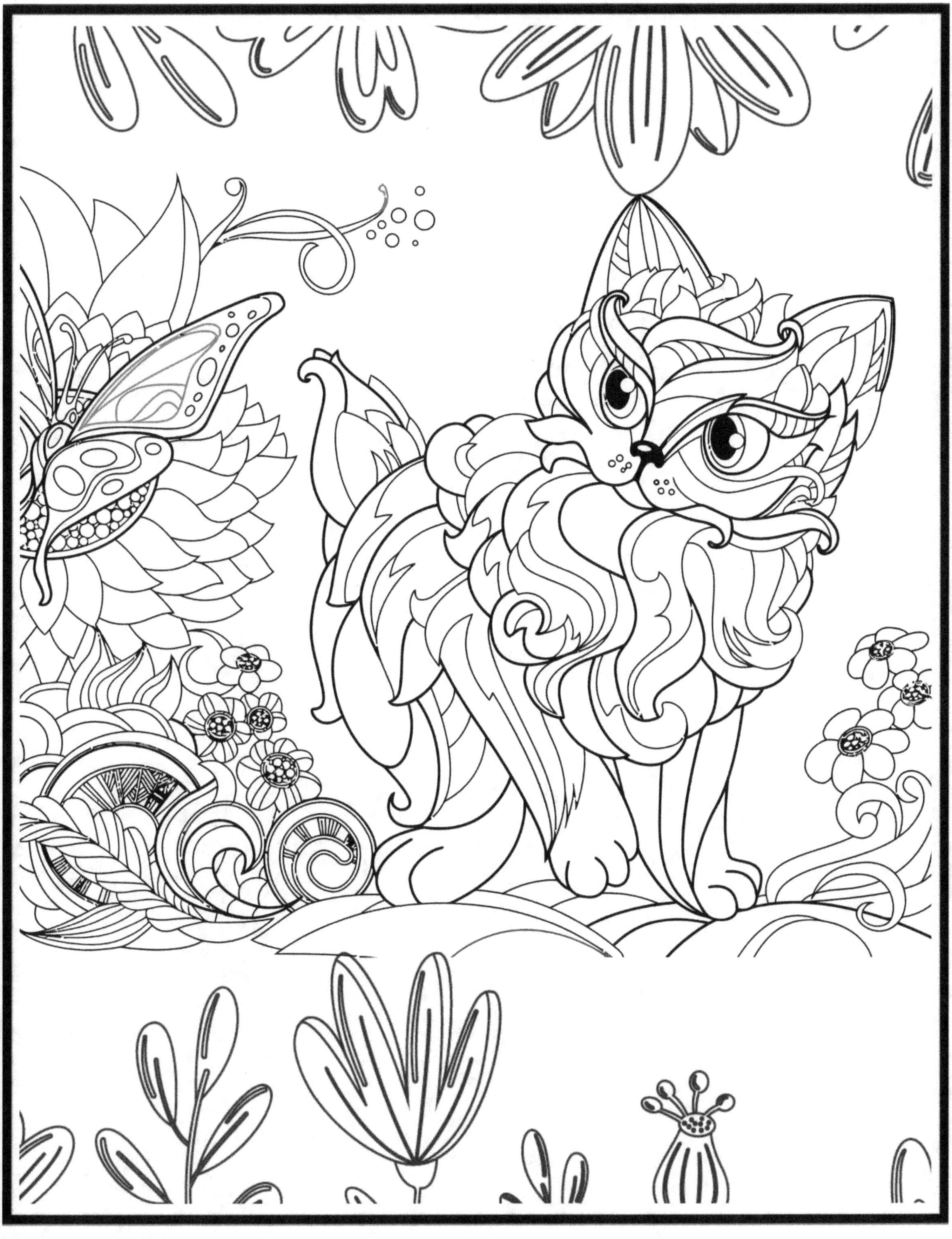

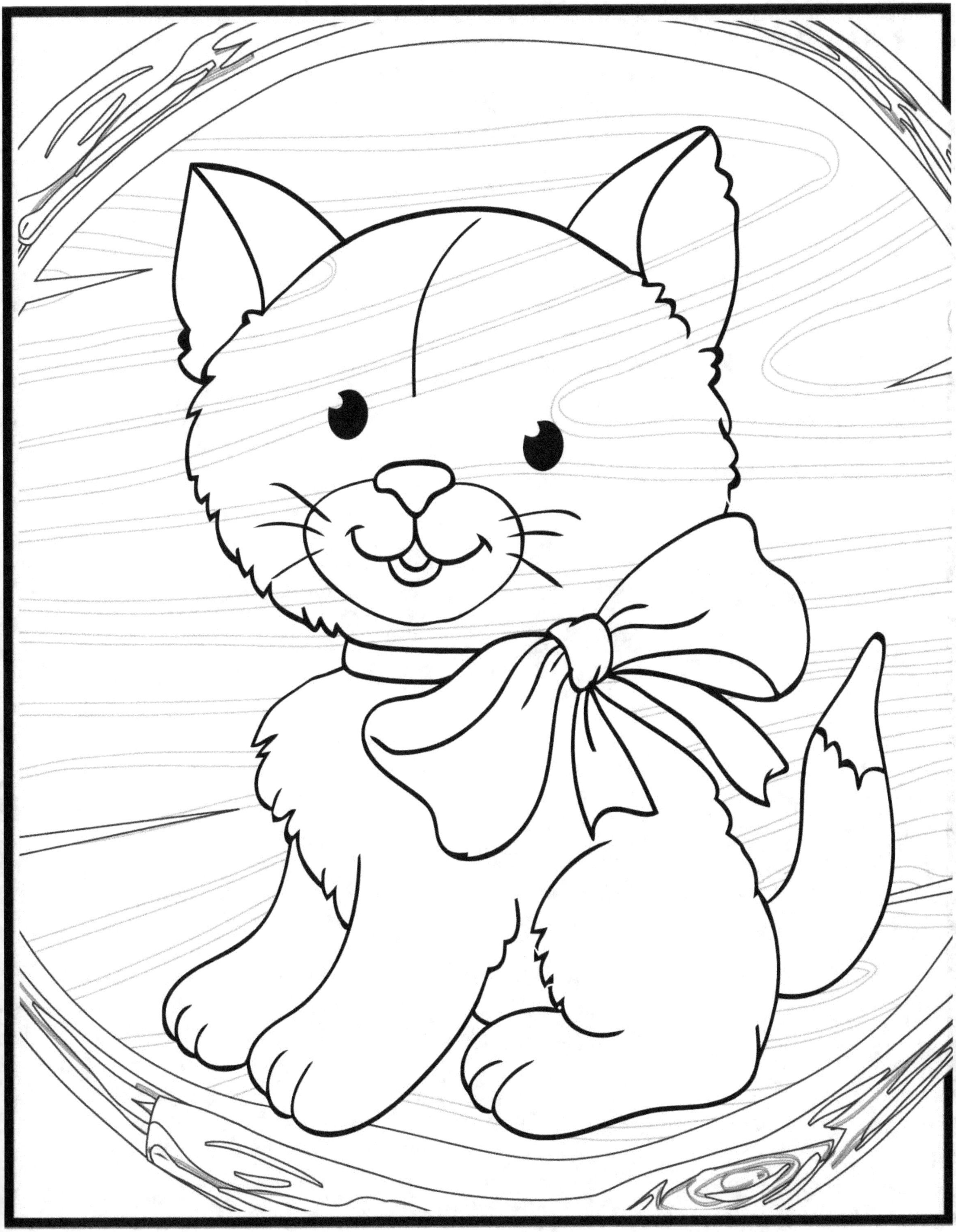

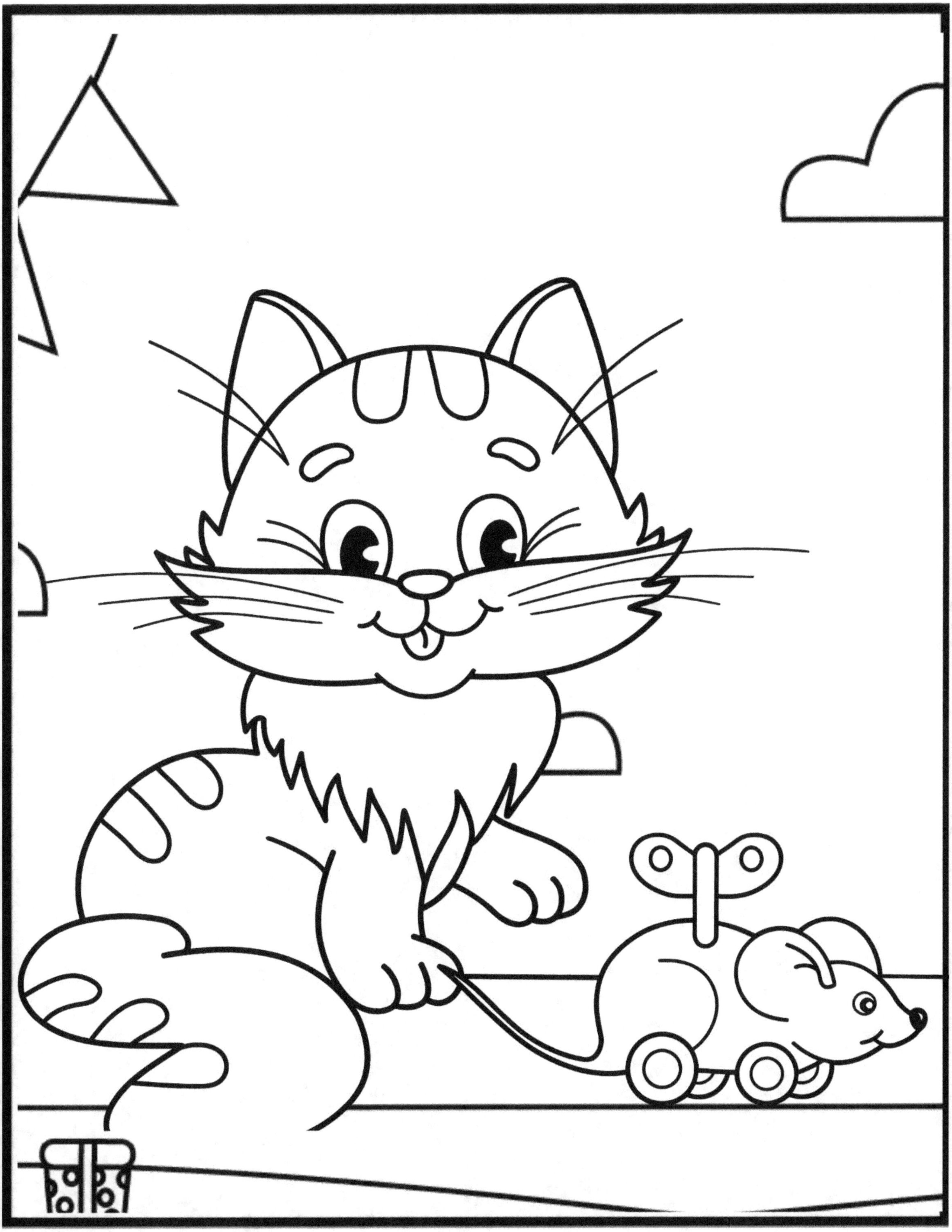

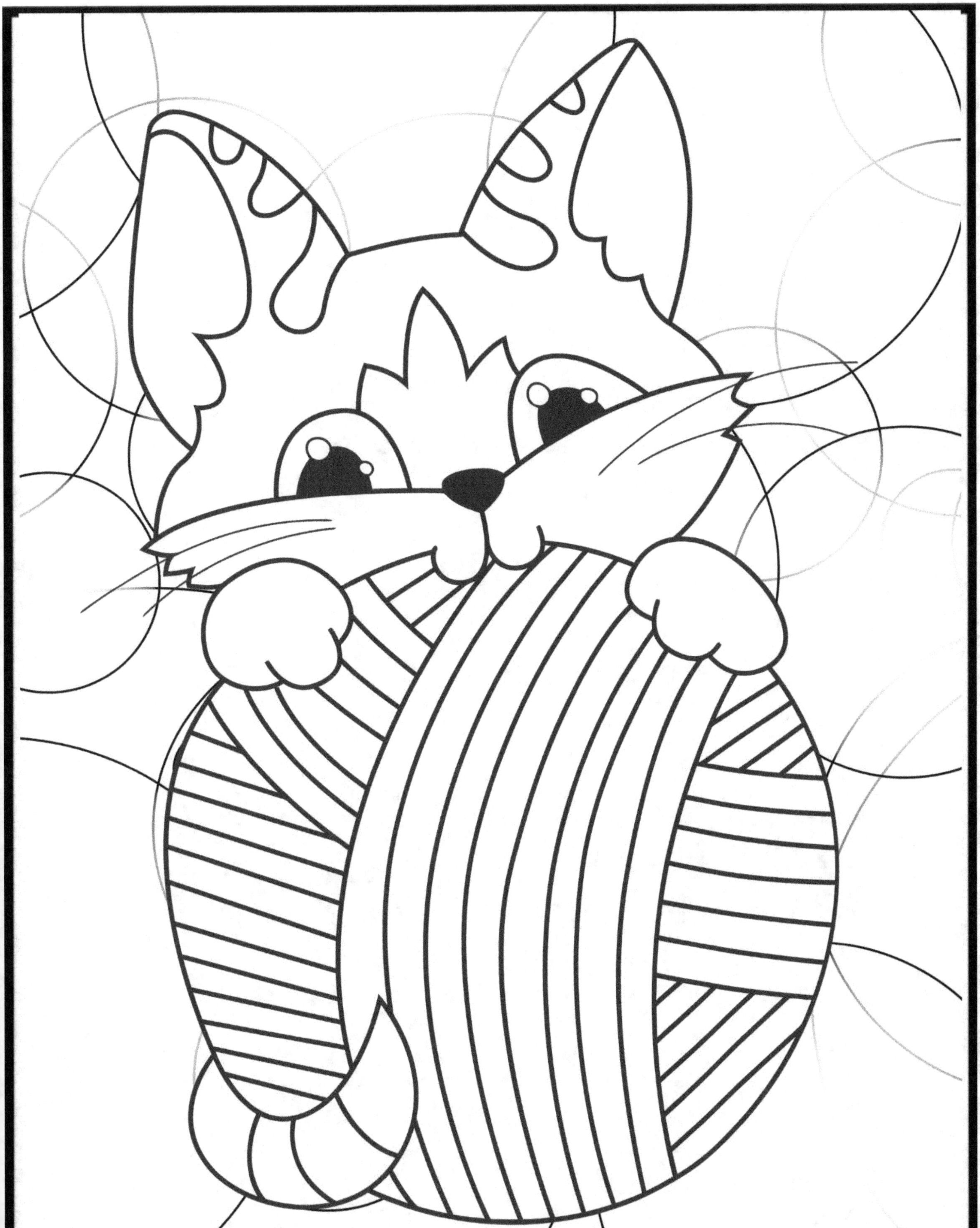

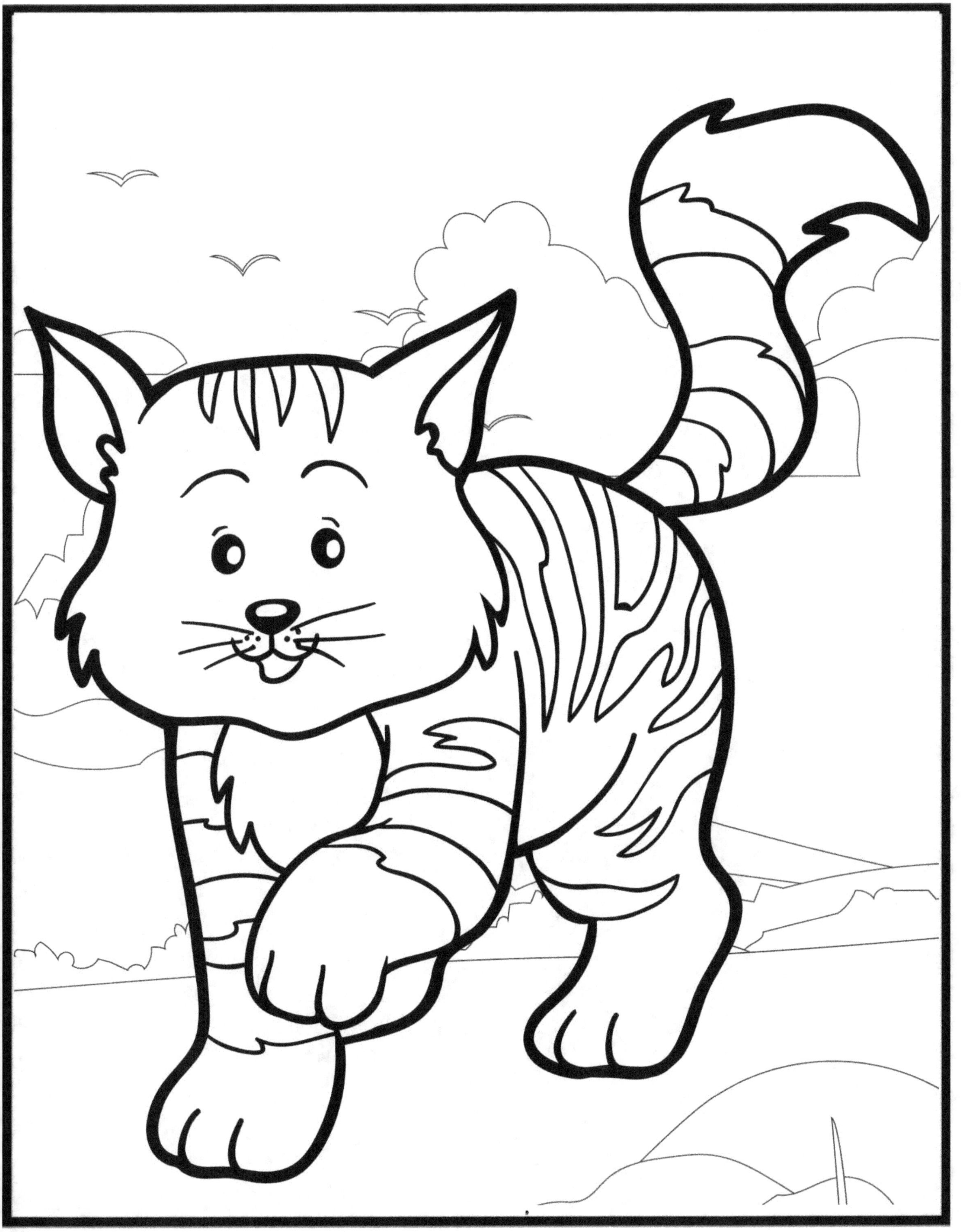

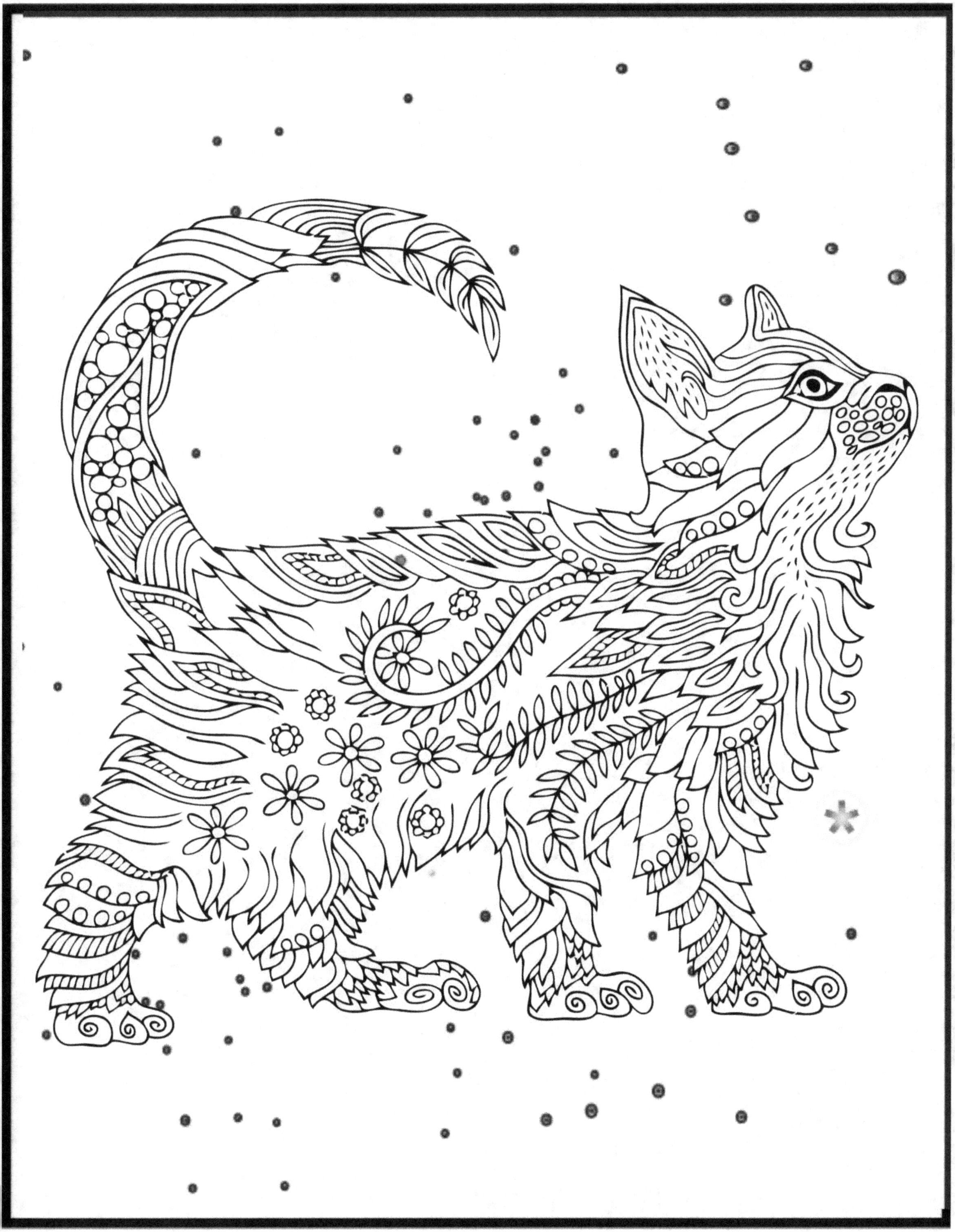

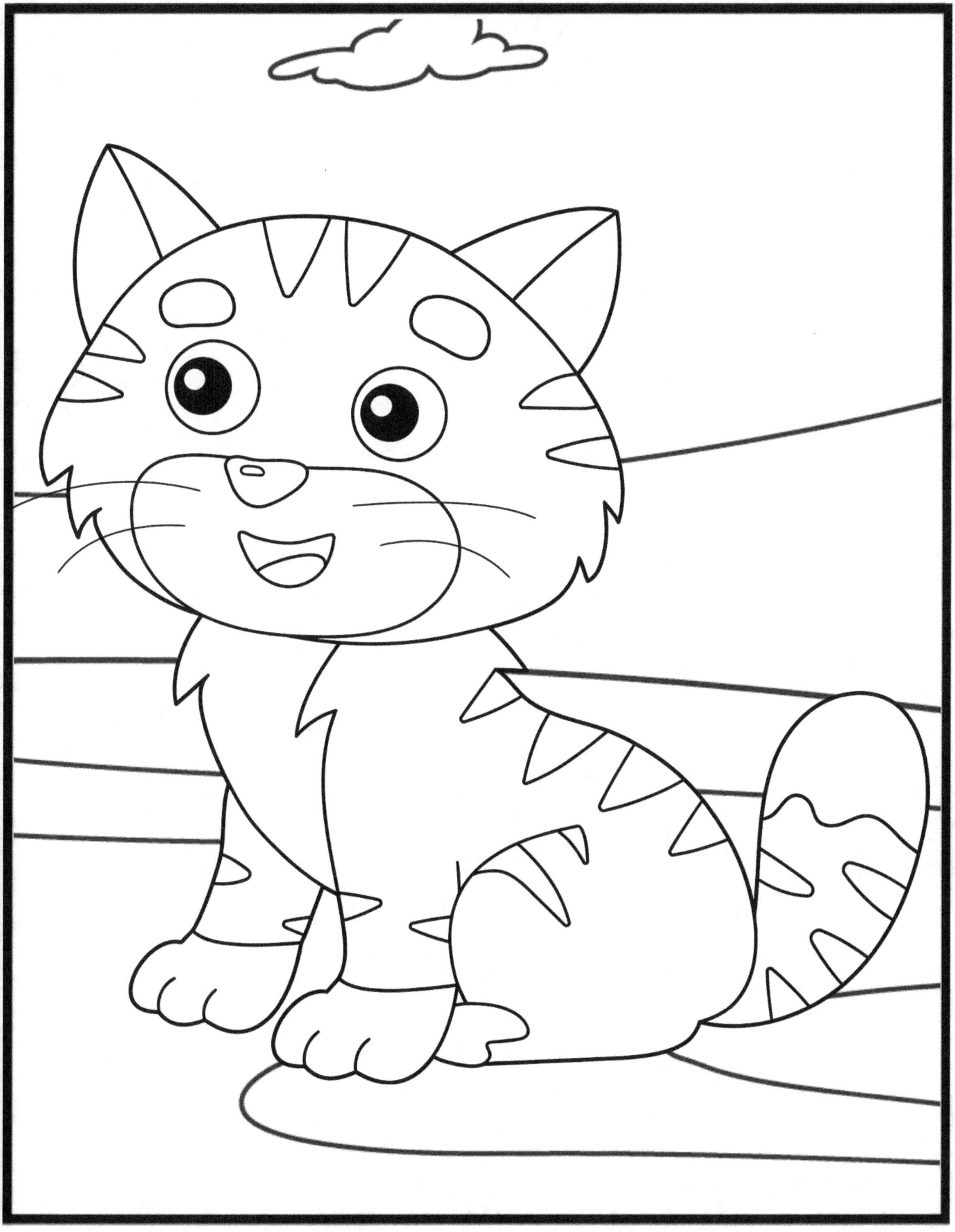

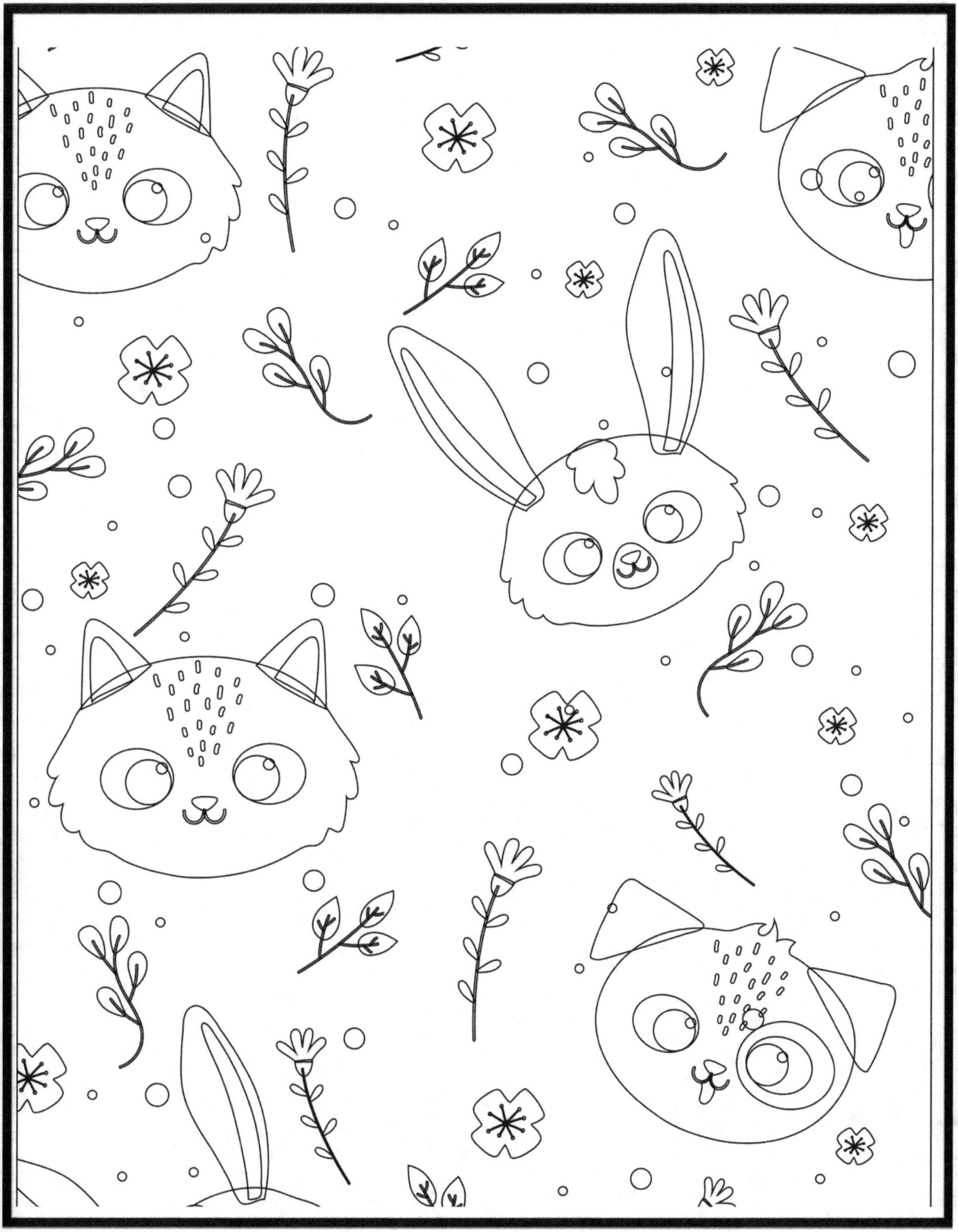

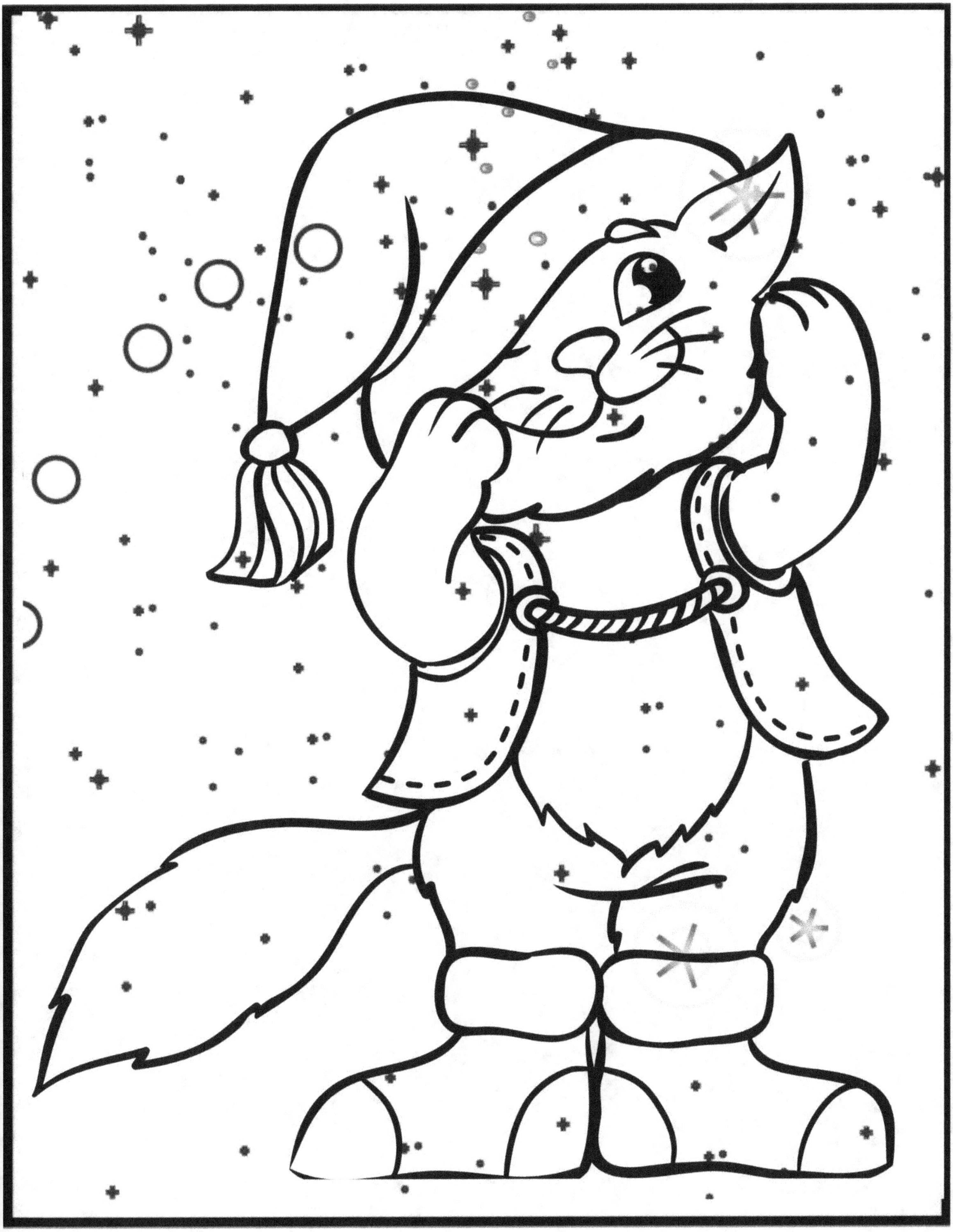

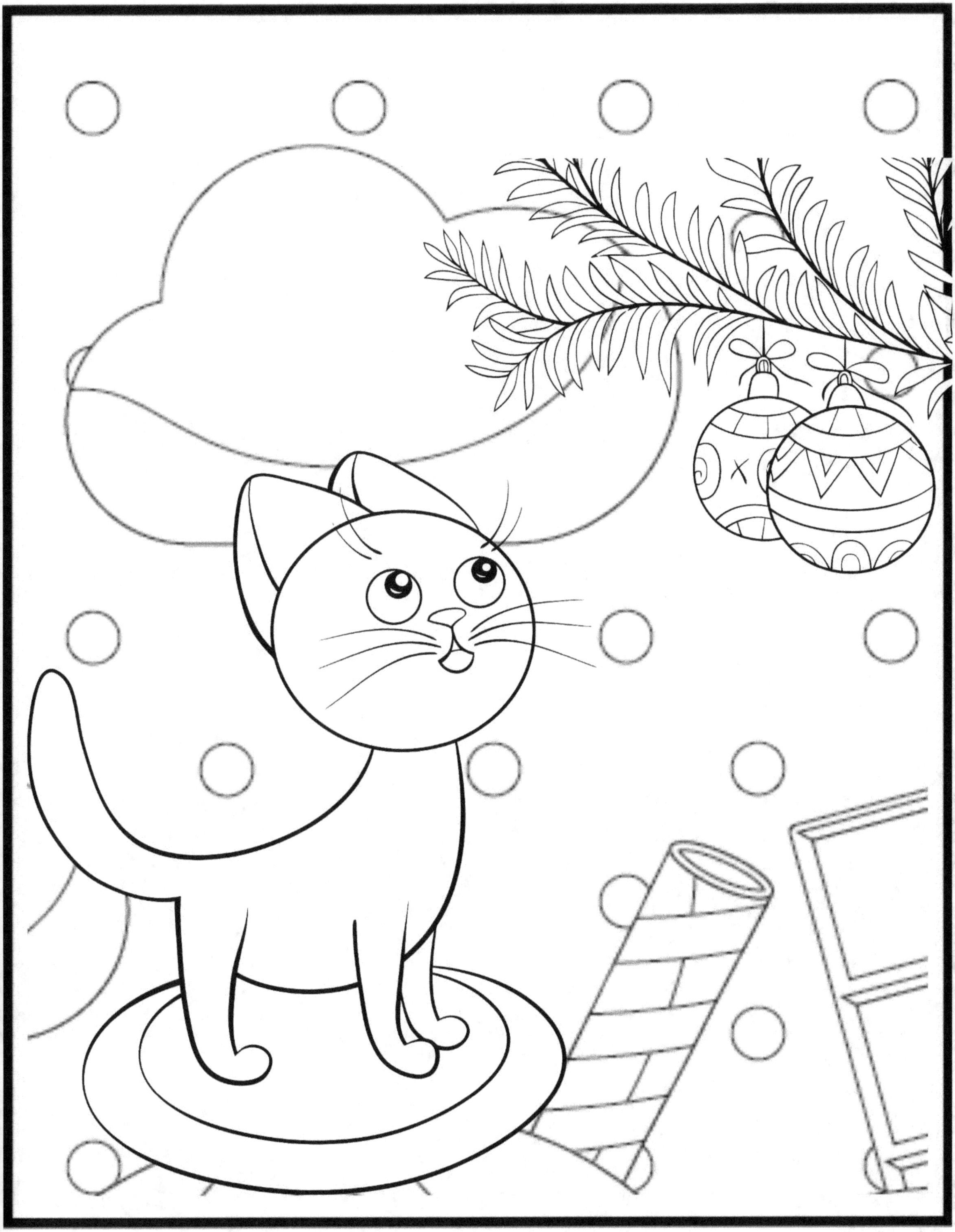

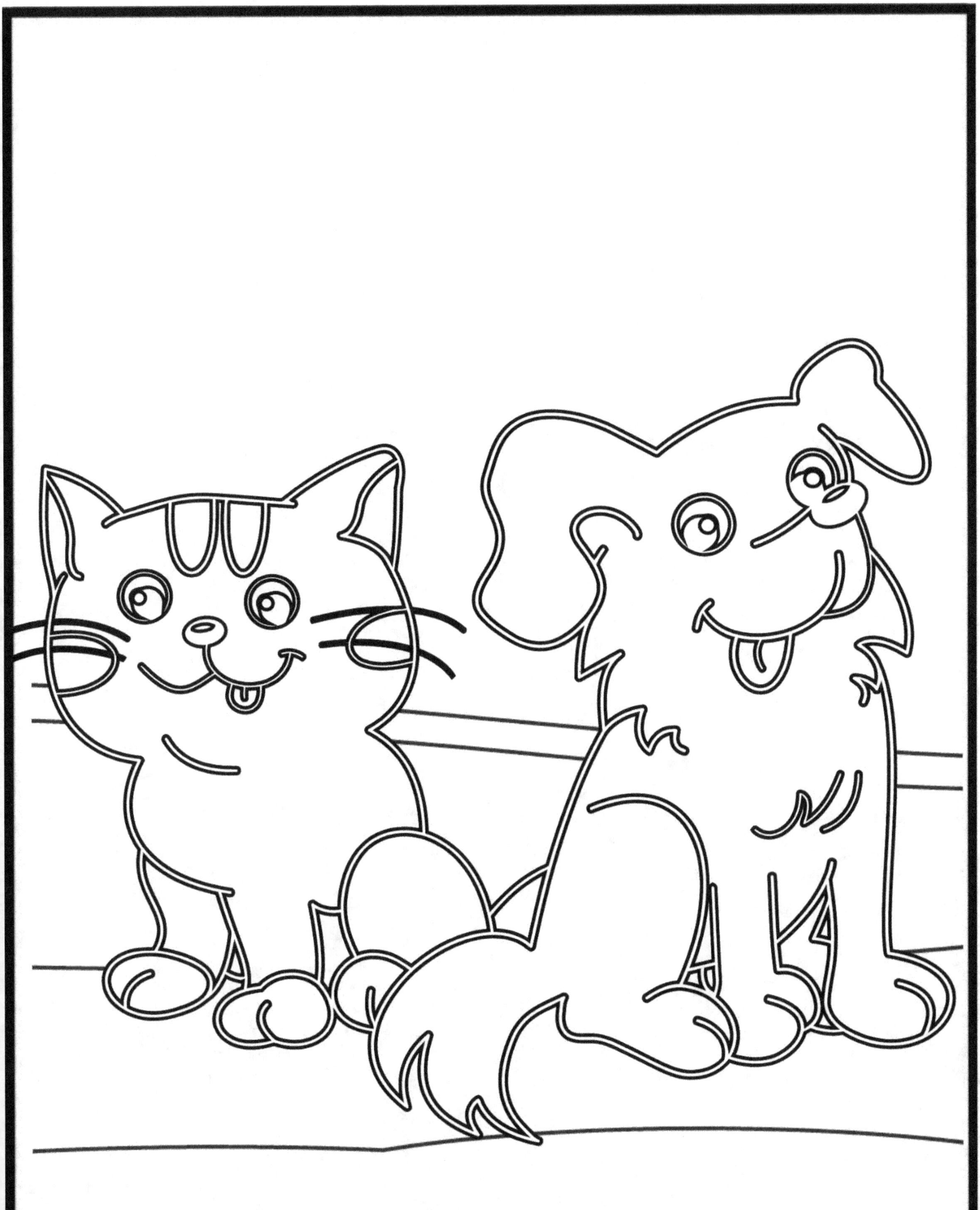

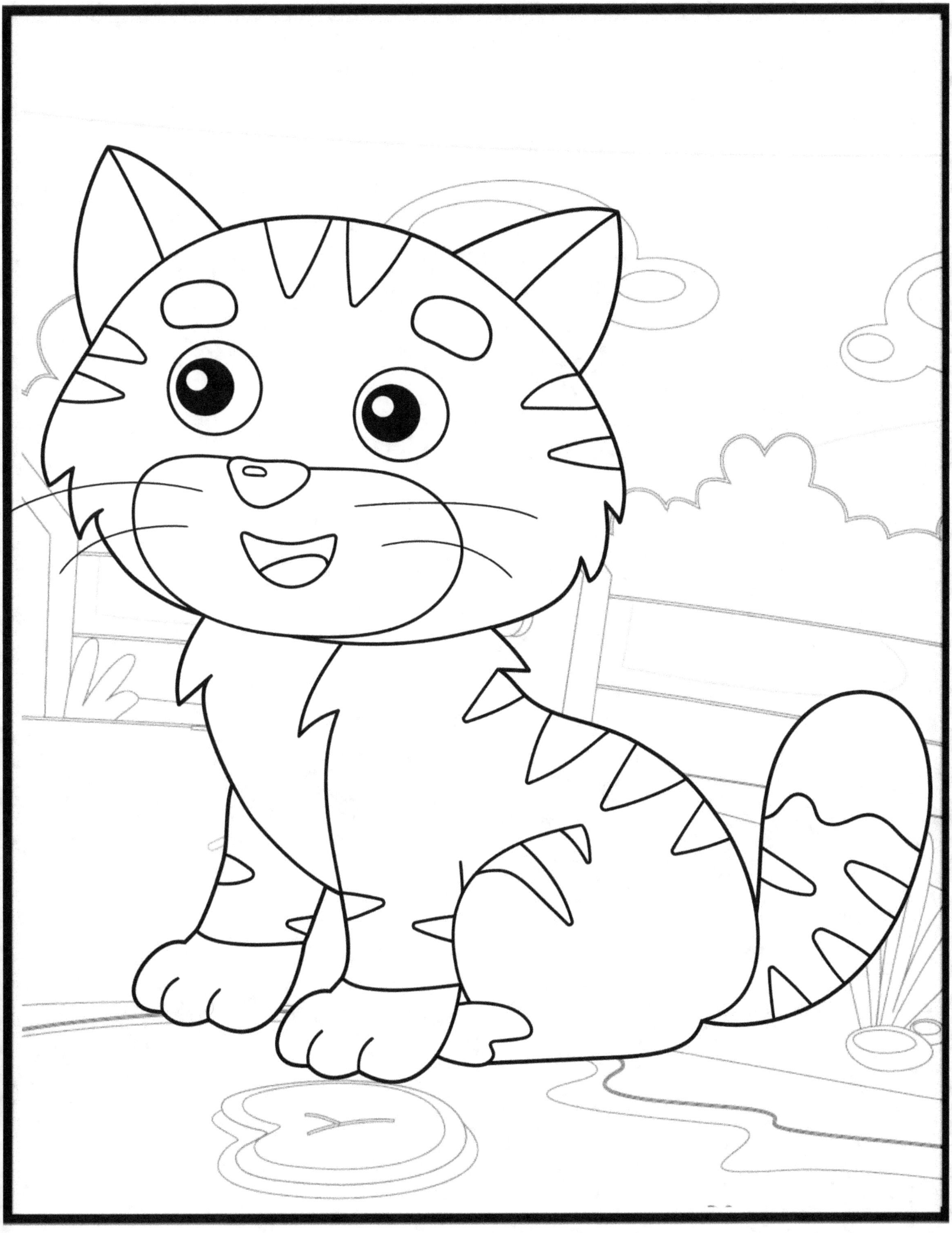

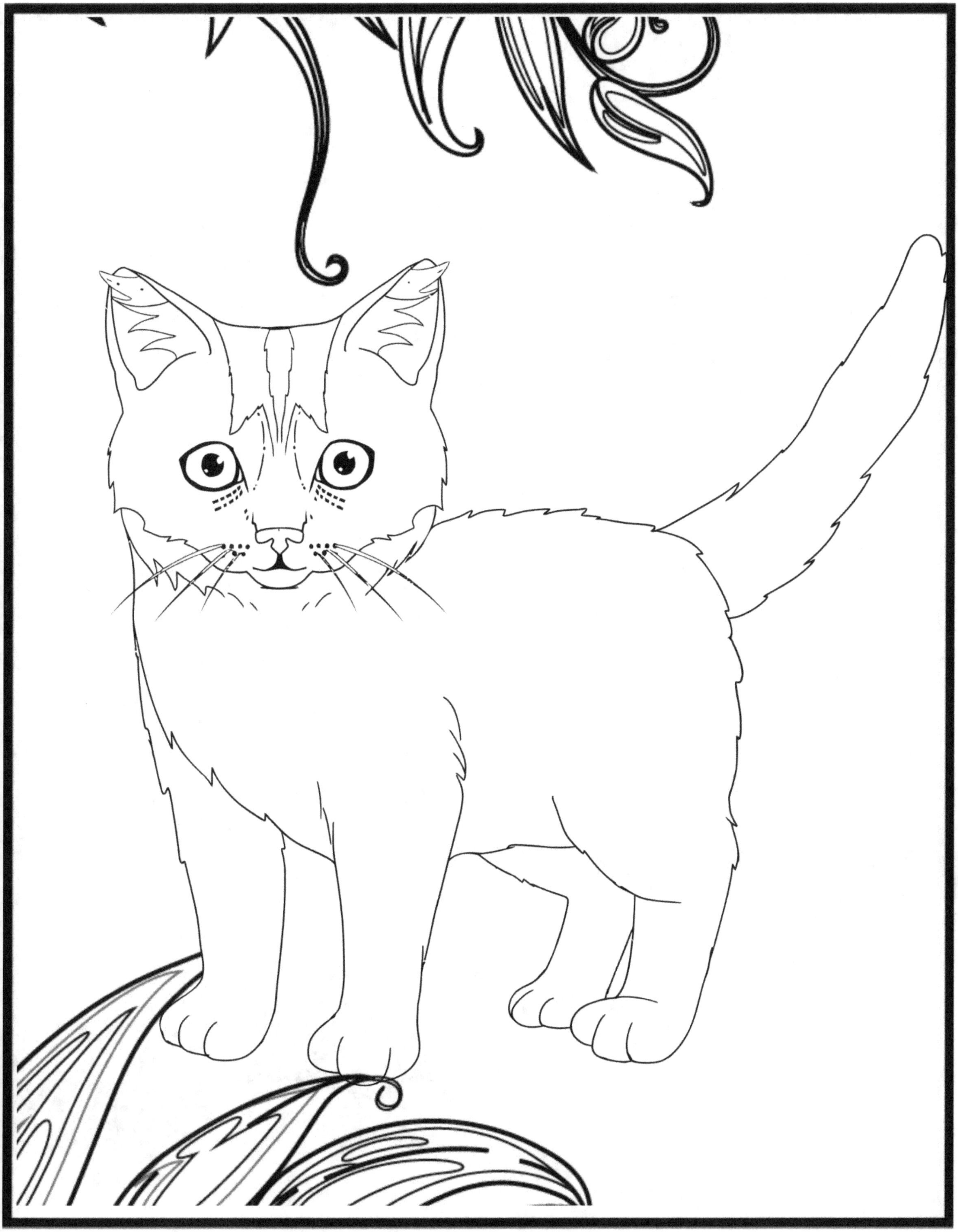

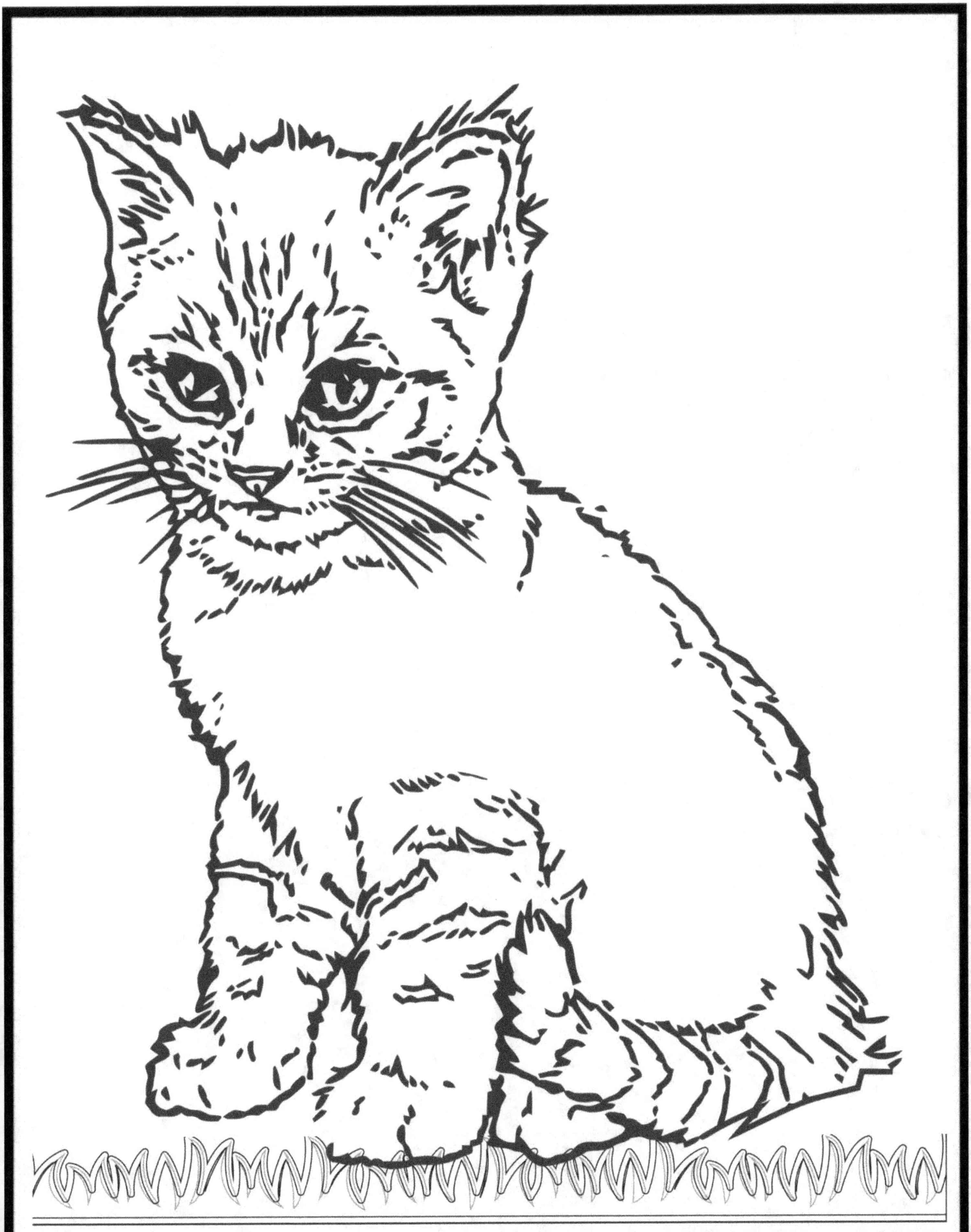

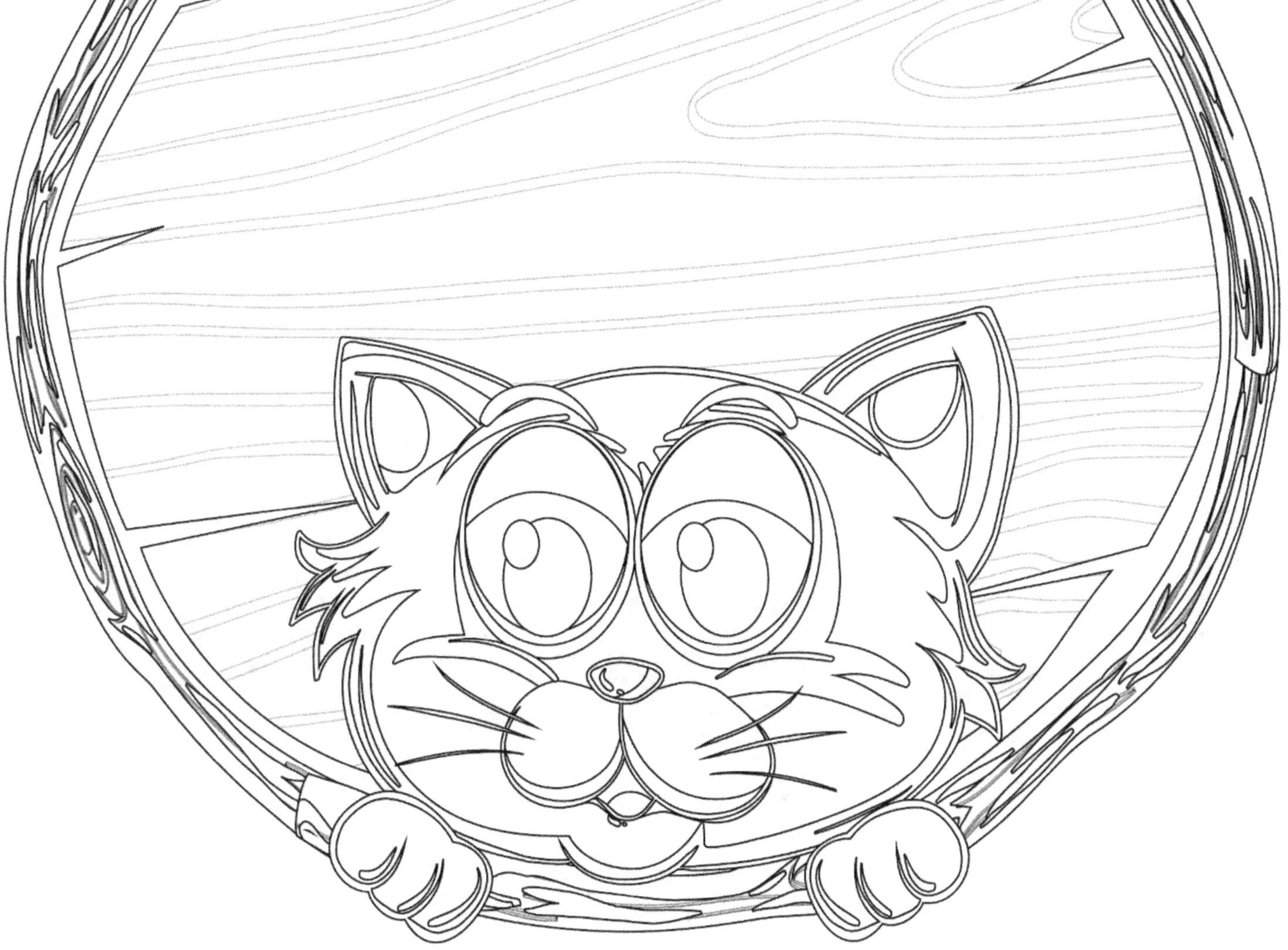

www.ingramcontent.com/pod-product-compliance
Lightning Source LLC
Chambersburg PA
CBHW080522220526
45465CB00006B/2566
* 9 7 9 8 7 4 9 7 4 2 8 3 1 *